HOW TO READ TOWNS & CITIES

HOW TO READ TOWNS & CITIES

A crash course in urban architecture

Jonathan Glancey

Bloomsbury Visual Arts
An imprint of Bloomsbury Publishing Plc

BLOOMSBURY
LONDON • OXFORD • NEW YORK • NEW DELHI • SYDNEY

Bloomsbury Visual Arts
An imprint of Bloomsbury Publishing Plc
Imprint previously known as A&C Black Visual Arts

50 Bedford Square
London
WC1B 3DP
UK

1385 Broadway
New York
NY 10018
USA

www.bloomsbury.com

BLOOMSBURY and the Diana logo are trademarks of Bloomsbury Publishing Plc

First published in Great Britain in 2016 by Bloomsbury Visual Arts

British Library Cataloguing-in-Publication Data

A catalogue record for this book is available from the British Library.

ISBN: 978-1-4742-1926-6

Colour origination by Ivy Press Reprographics

Printed in China

This book was conceived, designed and produced by

Ivy Press
210 High Street
Lewes, East Sussex
BN7 2NS, UK
www.ivypress.co.uk

PUBLISHER Susan Kelly
CREATIVE DIRECTOR Michael Whitehead
EDITORIAL DIRECTOR Tom Kitch
COMMISSIONING EDITOR Stephanie Evans
SENIOR PROJECT EDITOR Caroline Earle
EDITOR Jayne Ansell
DESIGN JC Lanaway
PICTURE RESEARCHER Katie Greenwood
ILLUSTRATOR Adam Hook

Front cover, background image:
Shutterstock/steve estvanik

Contents

INTROD

When is a town not a city and a city not a town? This question, or riddle, is unanswerable, a fact that will hold little appeal to the tidy-minded urbanist. The definition of what can constitute one or the other varies with governance around the world. In Britain, a town can become a city overnight if the monarch so decrees. In her Diamond Jubilee of 2012, Queen Elizabeth conjured three old towns Chelmsford (England), Perth (Scotland) and tiny St Asaph (Wales) into cities. Confusingly for visitors to Britain, London comprises two cities – London and Westminster – as well as a vast, doughnut-ring of suburbs.

There are no reliable definitions of a city or a town, and yet we know, as if instinctively, the essential and emotional difference between the two. Big or small, a city is the seat of regional power and administration and at least offers and expresses an intensity of life or cultural purpose different from that of towns.

Cities tend to change more quickly than towns, too. They are places people come to make their fortunes, to lose themselves, and even to change identities. They are where successive waves of immigrants arrive in search of work, shelter and, in certain parts of the world at least, freedom.

Knossos

Knossos was not large, yet the power of this city was amplified by the myths enveloping it: the labyrinth and the Minotaur.

UCTION

Traditionally, towns have been settlements largely devoted to local interests and particular trades and industries. This has made them powerful in their own right, and yet they are rarely centres of regional let alone national power. Where in Renaissance Italy, for example, there were many rival cities no bigger than contemporary English towns, these were first and foremost political entities, often fighting one another, for political rather than purely commercial gain.

The joy of reading towns and cities lies not so much in battling with definitions and semantics, but in their glorious variety. Identifying the elements of towns and cities of all eras worldwide and learning to understand these is a lifetime's joy to anyone with an eye for difference, a lust for travel and a keen sense of continuously unfolding urban and civic history.

City of London skyline
London is vast, its core remarkably small: the City, a place of modern myth that revolves around financial might.

Looking for Clues

The urban grid
The grid patterns of ancient Greek and Roman cities made rational and military sense. They imposed a sense of order on landscapes. They were easy to oversee and to extend in a neat and orderly fashion. They instilled a sense of purpose. This type of plan was to shape cities around the globe for many centuries.

Seen from afar or from on high, the patterns of very different towns and cities can be seen, if not necessarily understood. It is only down on the ground, in their grids or labyrinths of streets, that these all too human constructions reveal their identities and the visitor learns how to equate abstract, bird's-eye views with the life and character of individual towns and cities. Their characters and purposes, however, can be recognised by certain easily identifiable clues.

Many early cities, and again those of the Renaissance and Industrial eras – despotic regimes, too – have been laid out on geometric grids, evoking a sense of discipline and harmony, and expressing a sense of civic and civil order.

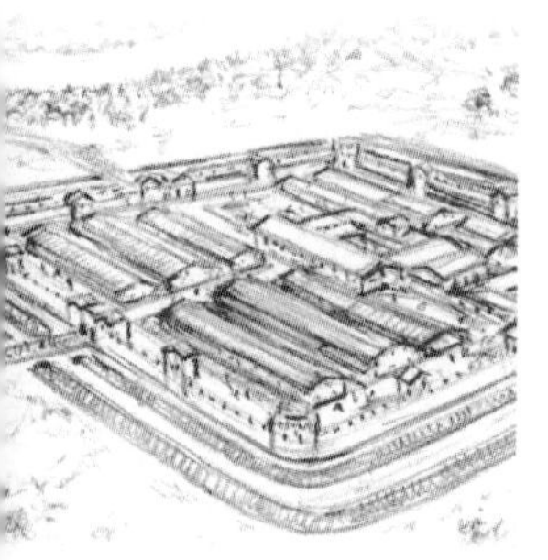

Urban sprawl (right)
The car changed everything. From the mid-20th century, towns and cities that might have begun with simple, geometric grid plans sprawled out to accommodate the all-conquering automobile. Beginning in the USA, this dynamic created its own patterns of loops, swirls and intersections best looked down on from skyscrapers.

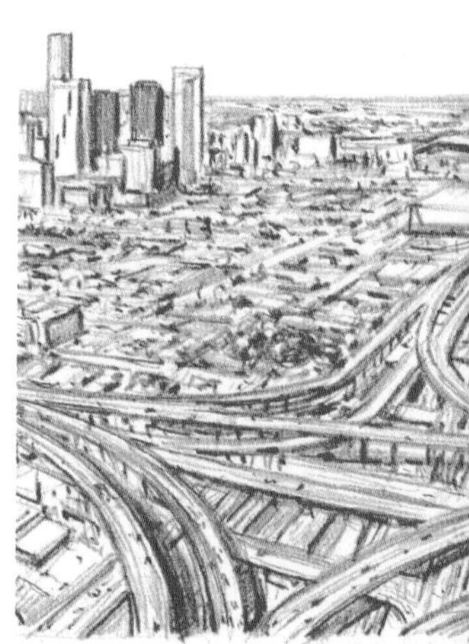

Squares

Whether a dust-covered central marketplace or a voluptuous Baroque piazza, the vast majority of towns and cities boast squares that draw visitors like bees to nectar or, by night, moths to a flame. These are their civic hearts, their cornerstones.

Commerce

Although globalism is changing this, each town and city has a distinct commercial character expressed historically through ports and quays, stockyards, office towers, banks, and in such compelling buildings as poetic medieval European cloth halls and prosaic 19th-century Manchester mills.

Skyline (below)

Adorned with cornucopias of towers, spires, domes or skyscrapers – and perhaps all of these – skylines offer an immediate sense of the life and character of a particular town or city: compare low, laid-back Copenhagen to high, intense Manhattan.

Poverty

Successful towns and cities have long been magnets for the rural poor and other immigrants. Whether in the guise of sprawling, low-rent suburbia, slums or shanty towns, this type of housing will only increase as global urbanisation grows apace.

PART ONE

The Grammar of Urban Architecture

Introduction

Mega city
The population of Greater Tokyo is much the same as that of Poland. This reflects the powerful economic and cultural draw of the Japanese capital, but also the fact that Japan is a mountainous country with precious little room for cities. Poland has space to breathe.

Cities vary in scale enormously. One of the very smallest, in terms of population, is St David's, Wales (pop, 1,800). At the other extreme, the metropolitan district of Tokyo is home to 36 million people. And, yet, however their scale is measured, cities tend to be composed of distinct and recognisable elements. Among these are central government buildings, royal palaces, cathedrals and other major places of worship along with munificent civic buildings and imposing streets and avenues. Not all cities will feature all the elements shown in the following pages. Some European cities lack cathedrals, for example, while there are many large towns boasting more imposing buildings than neighbouring cities.

Even so, cities grew up as the seats of power, the heart of unifying religions and – semantics aside – they are easily recognised, their identity perhaps even felt by visitors. And, although they do share a number of universal features – grand squares, an increasing intensity of architecture and activity towards their centres – cities come in many forms. The clustered skyscrapers of Chicago, Frankfurt and Shanghai spell the word 'city' loud and clear, and yet many of the world's great cities – Paris, Copenhagen, St Petersburg – are distinctly low-rise, although even these have witnessed the rise of modern towers on their peripheries.

City logos
Big and well-known cities feel the need to sell themselves to visitors and citizens alike with logos and nicknames – as if anyone needed reminding of their identity. Rome has stamped 'SPQR' (the Senate and People of Rome) on streets and buildings for more than 2,000 years.

Cities' plans vary greatly, too, as do those of towns. Some are laid out on nominally rational grids while others – London, for example – have grown up more loosely, or organically over the centuries.

As for details, cities are often identified by logos or coats-of-arms set into pavements, drain covers, the sides of buses and entrances to civic buildings. In Rome, the initials SPQR (the Senate and People of Rome) are happily unavoidable: age-old or brand new, cities like to proclaim their special status.

Central Core

The Acropolis, Athens
The Acropolis is perhaps the world's most famous citadel – the fortified core of a city – adorned with classical temples, notably the peerless 5th-century BCE Parthenon, built to glorify Athens during its 'golden age'. It has inspired rulers and their architects ever since.

Cities emerged in the Bronze Age not just when humans had settled in specific places and learned to farm systematically, but when such settlements produced a surplus of produce and there was time and the equivalent of money to invest in fortresses to protect themselves, temples to appease the gods who determined harvests and prosperity, and palaces for a new generation of kings whose duty it was to lead their people. Temples, palaces and forts formed the heart of cities.

Milan Cathedral

In Europe, cathedrals came to dominate city centres. Main roads and streets led inexorably to these daunting yet celebratory buildings that manifested and magnified the wealth, success and providence of their citizens. Set in the Piazza del Duomo, Milan Cathedral is a perfect example.

Tower of London

Rulers stamped their authority on city centres with castles expressing an unmistakable sense of power and control. In time of conflict, however, castles could protect citizens within their walls. William the Conqueror built the Tower of London after he seized the English throne in 1066.

Jaisalmer Fort, Rajasthan

At one time in its 850-year history, the entire population lived within the walls of Jaisalmer Fort, Rajasthan; the castle was synonymous with the city. Today, the population has spilt over into suburbs beneath its walls and it is the medieval fort itself that needs protection through conservation.

Palazzo Madama, Turin

From 1861, the Palazzo Madama, Turin, served as the first senate of the new Italian kingdom. Despite its 18th-century Baroque facade by Filippo Juvarra, the palace was built up from a medieval castle that in turn was developed from a Roman gateway that served as a fort.

Central Squares

Piazza San Marco, Venice
Piazza San Marco in Venice, an ideal city square, has been rebuilt over centuries. It faces the Byzantine domes of St Mark's Basilica, the sea to the south and an all but seamless enclosure of arcaded buildings shaping what appears to be one vast Venetian drawing room open to the sky.

The public square – *piazza, plaza, platz, ploshchad* – has been a key element of town and city centres from antiquity. These great meeting places developed either from market squares or were laid out to showcase palaces and temples. For centuries, they have been the focal point of commercial and public life, places of celebration and protest. The finest squares are often those that have been enclosed by elegant, rhythmic buildings, surrounded by colonnades and adorned with fountains, civic monuments and cafes.

Red Square, Moscow

Moscow's Red Square was the original point of landing for goods and visitors to the Russian city. Dividing the Kremlin, a royal citadel, from the commercial quarters of the city, it has hosted great religious processions, and from 1917 parades of Soviet military might be overseen from Lenin's Mausoleum.

Djemaa el-Fna, Marrakesh

Djemaa el-Fna, the great central square of Marrakesh, retains its theatrical and pungent medieval atmosphere. Flanked by mosques, palaces, parade grounds, souqs and gardens, it has been a place of execution, eating, enterprise and entertainment. Fully alive, it is also a World Heritage Site.

Times Square, New York

Jammed with automobiles for decades, the vast traffic intersection known since 1904 as Times Square has been transformed into a pedestrian plaza. Flanked by neon adverts, theatres, music halls and sleaze, this hugely popular New York gathering place has become what it always wanted to be: a true city square.

Medieval square, Bernkastel-Kues

The medieval square at the heart of Bernkastel-Kues, a wine-growing town that straddles the River Moselle, is on one level a picture-book German experience. It is also the hub of thriving local commerce in a region where independent shops and family businesses prosper in a perfect setting.

Gateways & Walls

Talipach Gate, Bukhara
The image of the walled town has been handed down through folklore and fairy tales. For centuries, caravanserais making their way along Central Asia's Silk Road would stop at monumental gateways like this – the Talipach Gate at Bukhara, Uzbekistan – to pay levies and taxes before entering protective walls.

Towns and cities have often been surrounded by walls and entered through grand gateways. While protecting citizens, these have also been ways of expressing confidence, identity and a sense of permanence in a transient world. Many were demolished as political power was centralised in most countries around the world. In a spirit of Romanticism, however, city walls were often restored in the 19th century, while new forms of symbolic gateways have emerged as a substitute for muscular towers and portcullises.

Brandenburg Gate, Berlin
From the Renaissance, monumental gateways inspired by ancient precedent became de rigueur in European cities. The imposing Greek Doric-style Brandenburg Gate, Berlin (1791), fronted Unter den Linden, the avenue leading to the Prussian royal palace. Closed during the Cold War, in 1989 it became a gateway to a re-unified Germany.

Roman gateway, Palmyra
Roman towns and cities boasted numerous monumental gateways. This early-3rd-century CE example at Palmyra, a once wealthy oasis town in Syria, is the heroic link between stretches of a kilometre-long colonnaded avenue, complete with temples, baths, a theatre, markets and shops.

City walls, Ávila
The walls of the Castilian city Ávila are punctuated by no fewer than 88 circular towers. They were built, beginning in 1090, using ancient Roman stones wherever possible, to protect the city during the Moorish invasion of Spain. The cities of Salamanca and Segovia built similar walls, but those of Ávila survive intact.

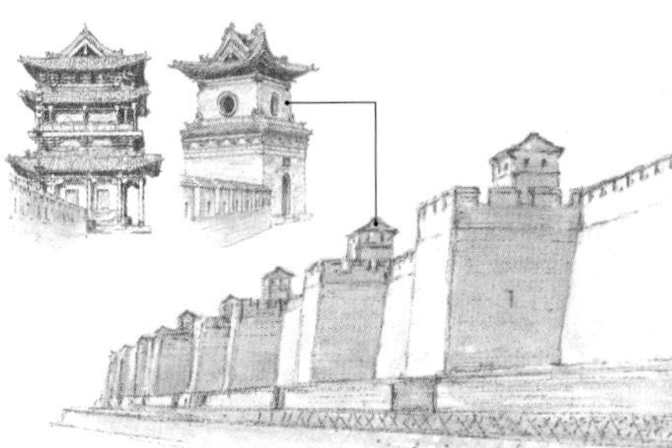

City walls, Pingyao
Chinese cities were often surrounded by impressive walls. Those of Pingyao, Shanxi Province, were developed from early times and through the Ming dynasty (1368–1644). Six kilometres (3.7 miles) of 12-m (39-ft) high walls are pierced by six powerful, yet highly ornamented gates and crowned with 72 watchtowers.

Principal Streets

Champs-Élysées, Paris
The Champs-Élysées is a commanding Parisian avenue, 1.9-km (1.2-miles) long and 70-m (230-ft) wide, connecting Place de la Concorde to the Arc de Triomphe. Lined with clipped horse-chestnut trees, it was designed by André le Nôtre, landscape architect to Louis XIV.

Grand streets and avenues lead to and from important city landmarks like enormous open-air corridors. These are the main arteries of the city: life and traffic courses along them. Where power has been centralised in self-important capital cities, such streets are often inordinately long and wide, planned for pomp, promenade and procession as well commerce and entertainment. Many of these are lined with impressive buildings. Some end in impressive architectural vistas; others appear to stretch as far as the eye can see.

Piazza del Popolo, Rome

The Via Flaminia, an ancient Roman road and the main entry to Rome itself before the railways, leads into the theatrical Piazza del Popolo with its twin Baroque churches and Egyptian obelisk. From here three main streets spear out like the prongs of a trident to key points of the city.

Rajpath, New Delhi

Originally King's Way, New Delhi's Rajpath is a hugely impressive avenue beginning at the India Gate war memorial and continuing up Raisina Hill to Rashtrapati Bhavan (the former Viceroy's House). This is the work of the British architect Edwin Lutyens. It comes truly alive with opulent national and military parades.

Pa Bjerget, Copenhagen

It is just a short walk along Pa Bjerget in Copenhagen's Bispebjerg district to the imposing, and slightly frightening, Grundtvig's Church (1927–40), yet the grandeur of the planning and architecture makes this street seem heroic. In the opposite direction, the eye is led along an avenue through a parkland cemetery.

Fifth Avenue, New York

As much a legend as an urban thoroughfare, Fifth Avenue dates from 1811 when the grid plan of Manhattan was commissioned. It leads from Washington Square North to 142 Street, Harlem, taking in the Empire State Building, famous hotels, department stores, the 'Museum Mile' and processions galore.

Civic Buildings

Viceroy's House, New Delhi
Edwin Lutyens' Viceroy's House, New Delhi, (1912–29) is a masterpiece of British imperial design; since 1947, it has been equally feted as the home of the presidents of an independent India. Its design fuses English classicism, Indian motifs and the architecture of imperial Rome.

From the beginning cities and towns have been centres of local, regional and state governance. Surprisingly small towns boast imposing civic buildings, while parliamentary and government buildings of capital cities are often referred to as palaces even in an era of republics. Designed by the most renowned architects of their day, these are sights that tourists flock to see. Governments occupy whole quarters of cities and these are usually distinct from commercial districts, just as they were in the ancient world.

Norwich City Hall

Norwich City Hall is a handsome and beautifully crafted 1930s building designed in a contemporary Scandinavian classical style by Charles Holloway James and Stephen Rowland Pierce. It overlooks the city's busy daily market and so connects Norwich's trade and commerce to its politics and governance.

The Alvorada Palace, Brasilia

Oscar Niemeyer, a 20th-century Brazilian modernist, proved how it was possible to shape a presidential palace in strikingly Modern forms. The Alvorada Palace (1958) was the first government building constructed in the new Brazilian capital, Brasilia. It shimmers on a peninsula overlooking Lake Paranoá.

Town hall, Sabaudia

Its lofty, if austere, town hall dominates the 1930s Italian new town of Sabaudia. Laid out like a miniature version of ancient Rome, this is one of a cluster of towns commissioned by Benito Mussolini and built in record time on the drained, and formerly malarial, Pontine Marshes.

Camden City Hall, South Carolina

The City Hall of Camden, South Carolina, looks 18th century, but it dates from 1956. The design blends in with the historic buildings of this Georgian town. It also shows how the governmental architecture of the most democratic New World towns often harks back to ancient Greece and Rome.

Major Commercial Buildings

Guild houses, Antwerp
These delightful late-16th-century guild houses, renovated in the 19th century and fronting the Grote Markt, stand cheek-by-jowl with Antwerp's historic City Hall. Their lavish designs demonstrate in no uncertain fashion the wealth and civic power of archers, grocers, tailors and carpenters.

Invariably, towns have been founded on trade and commerce, while cities have begun as political and religious centres around which trade has grown. Commercial buildings tend to dominate the skylines of contemporary cities; cathedrals and palaces have all but vanished in their obliterating shadows. And, yet, in many historic towns, the architecture of commerce – of guilds, merchants and banks as well as that of tithe barns and storehouses – rivalled that of the church and civic power.

Wool Hall, Lavenham

The wool trade in 15th-century Suffolk was akin to religion: the wool guild, founded in Lavenham in 1529 called itself the Guild of Corpus Christi. Its timber-framed hall became the centre of local business. A prison and workhouse in less prosperous times, it is a National Trust property today.

Cloth Hall, Ypres

Completed in 1304, the cathedral-like Cloth Hall at Ypres was one of the most ambitious of all medieval commercial buildings. With its prominent tower, housing a carillon of 49 bells, its presence was unmissable. Devastated during the First World War, it was lovingly rebuilt between 1928 and 1967.

Ca' D'Oro, Glasgow

Glasgow's wrought iron Ca' D'Oro (1872) was designed as a furniture warehouse, and yet its style was based on that of the 15th-century Venetian palazzo, Ca' d'Oro. Here was a very cultured commercial building linking the mercantile power of medieval Venice to 19th-century Scotland.

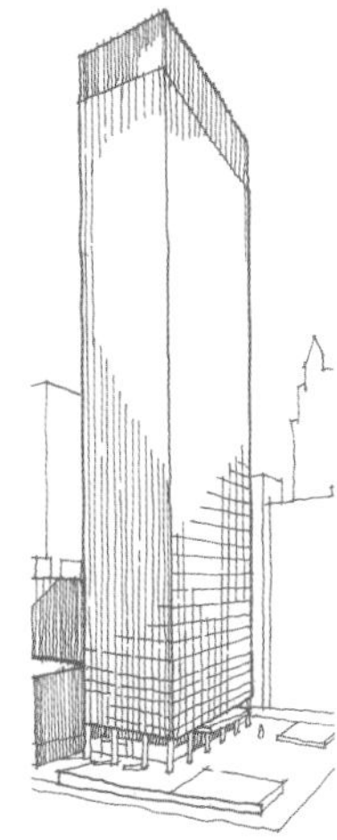

Seagram Building, New York

The Seagram Building (1958) set back in splendid isolation from New York's Park Avenue set the tone for countless modern office buildings around the world. Designed by Ludwig Mies van der Rohe, it was built with expensive materials and has been treated by most architects with reverence ever since.

Universities & Colleges

Lomonosov Moscow State University
Commanding views of central Moscow from their hilltop location, the vast and lofty central buildings of Lomonosov Moscow State University form a city within the city. The 'wedding cake' tower was Europe's tallest building from 1953 to 1990

The first universities, emerging in Europe from the late 11th century, were closely associated with the Church. From the Renaissance their concerns were increasingly secular, and during the 19th century they became driving forces along with local colleges and institutes of scientific discovery and industrialisation. Factories of the intellect, these seats of learning were not only of immense value, but they also nurtured inspiring architecture, campuses and entire quarters of the towns and cities they grew up in.

University of Virginia, Charlottesville

The original campus of the University of Virginia, Charlottesville, was designed by Thomas Jefferson (third president of the United States) in the guise of a miniature ancient Rome, complete with its own Pantheon and colonnaded streets in parkland to the west of the city centre.

University of Oxford

The distant view of Oxford prompted the Victorian poet Matthew Arnold to evoke 'that sweet city with her dreaming spires'. The view survives and, from this distance, central Oxford – its streets, lanes and lyrical architecture – remains synonymous with its university founded in 1167.

University of Bologna

The University of Bologna, Europe's first, dates from 1088. Its first purpose-built accommodation was the Palazzo dell'Archiginnasio commissioned by Charles Borromeo, a leading figure in the Counter Reformation, and completed in 1563. The university has grown around its 16th-century courtyard in the heart of the city.

The Wills Memorial Building, Bristol

The Wills Memorial Building (1925) looms high above the streets of Bristol. A gift of the Wills family – owners of the Imperial Tobacco Company – it was designed by Sir George Oatley in a late-flowering Gothic Revival style, and in the spirit of medieval universities.

Water

Liverpool Pier Head
The pity today is that few ships tie up alongside Liverpool's magnificent Pier Head. Here, on the site of the 18th-century George's Dock, on the River Mersey, the 'Three Graces' – the Royal Liver, Cunard and Port of Liverpool Buildings – rose shortly before the First World War.

Towns and cities have made use of water, through both necessity and design, since the very first were constructed some 7,500 years ago. Harbours by gulfs, seas and tidal rivers spelt havens for ships and thus ports and trade. As trade grew, so did ambitious urban plans, showcase buildings and waterfront skylines that have become symbols of the cities they adorn. Where water dried up or existed in insufficient quantities, and aqueducts were not an option, towns and cities vanished.

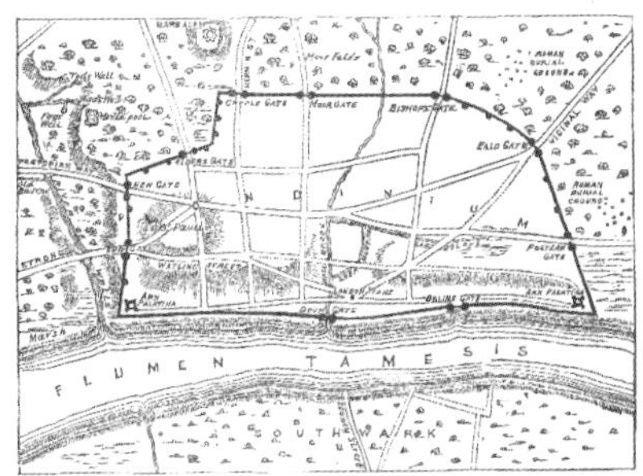

Roman dock, London
Founded in 47 CE, Londinium was not the capital of Roman Britain, but its major port and commercial hub. The tides of the River Thames sped ships from this sheltered haven to the sea. Sacked, however, by the British queen Boudicca, it was rebuilt as a planned Roman town from 60 CE.

Albert Dock, Liverpool
Liverpool's fortune was made with seaborne trade. The city's wealth was evident in its fine streets and Georgian buildings; yet as majestic as any of these was Albert Dock (1846), a supreme example of 19th-century mercantile architecture, and home today to hotels, restaurants and the Tate Liverpool.

The Arsenale, Venice
The military prowess, fortune and fame of the long-lived Venetian Republic owed very much indeed to the Arsenale di Venezia, the world's largest manufacturing complex before the Industrial Revolution. Ships, guns and munitions were produced in large numbers here. The Arsenale spreads across a sixth of the city.

Grand Canal, Trieste
Trieste is a wealthy Italian seaport. From 1382 to 1918, it was part of the Hapsburg Empire. The monumental axis leading from the sea along the Grand Canal to the Neo-Classical church of Sant' Antonio Nuovo, based on the Pantheon with Greek flavouring, is one of Europe's best-looking streets.

Water

Basilica Cistern, Istanbul
The sublime Basilica Cistern, resembling an underground Roman temple complete with 12 rows of 28 nine-metre (30-ft) high marble columns, was commissioned by the Emperor Justinian I in the 6th century to supply water to the Great Palace of Constantinople. Today, it is one of Istanbul's most treasured tourist attractions.

Essential to life, water has long been celebrated in towns and cities. Joyous fountains, heroic aqueducts, lively, gurgling gargoyles and spouts animate buildings, streets, squares and landscapes stretching out to hills beyond. Even when water serves essential services, whether for drinking, fire-fighting, sanitation or washing, the buildings it courses through have often been designed in the guises of palaces or cathedrals. From drinking fountains, horse troughs, gutters, underground cisterns and pumping stations, water has done much to shape urbanity.

Fontana Santa Sabina, Rome

There are said to be 280 fountains in Rome. The frightening masked face of the Fontana Santa Sabina, a 5th-century basilica, gushes water into an ancient basin. It was designed by Giacomo della Porta, one of the architects of St Peter's, which can be seen from this unforgettable fountain.

Craig Goch dam

Craig Goch (1904), central Wales, is the uppermost of five wondrous dams that have channelled drinking water to the inland city of Birmingham, 117 km (73 miles) away, from the beginning of the 20th century. A spectacular feat of engineering, it is also a triumphant example of municipal Birmingham Baroque design.

Crossness Pumping Station, London

The Prince of Wales and the Archbishop of Canterbury were among the dignitaries at the opening of Crossness Pumping Station to the far east of London in 1865. The architecture of this thrilling cathedral of sewage shows just how important its role was in the life of the Victorian city.

Thames Embankment, London

The noble Thames Embankment, built by Sir Joseph Bazalgette from 1862, changed the face of central London. It was built on a heroic scale, concealing huge sewers, and an underground railway, and taking the city's waste miles to the east. It played a major role in the eradication of cholera.

Transport

St Pancras Station, London
As medieval cloth halls adopted the architectural lineaments of cathedrals, so did some of the most ambitious 19th-century railway stations. St Pancras (1868–73), fronted by the Midland Grand Hotel, is a Gothic Revival hymn to the high Victorian railway age.

Transport is as necessary to towns and cities as water. Until the arrival of railways, it was not always well organised. Julius Caesar complained about the noise and chaos of ox carts rumbling through congested Roman streets at night. Railways brought timetables, reliability and the ability to transport goods quickly, so that, say, fresh fish from the Highlands could be served within hours in London restaurants. Building materials moved easily too, so towns and cities started to adopt one another's physical characteristics.

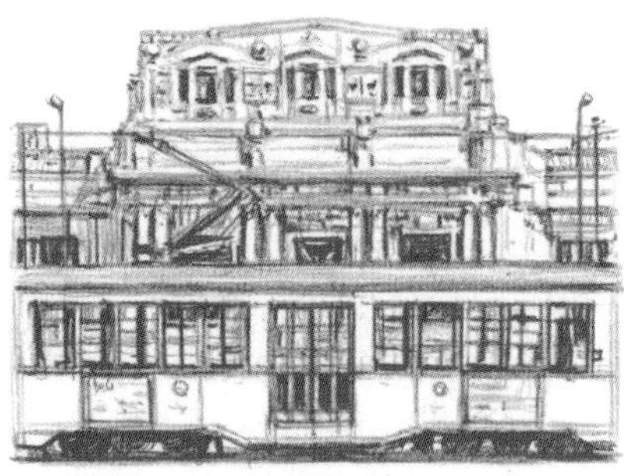

Milan tram and railway station

The sight and sound of trams makes cities special and all the more urban. Since 1881, Milan's tram routes have radiated from Piazza del Duomo. A part of the urban streetscape, many date from the early 1930s and have become as treasured as the historic buildings they rumble past.

London Underground

The 'bullseye' station signs of the London Underground devised by the calligrapher Edward Johnston between 1913 and 1917 became a symbol of the city itself. The system's chief executive, Frank Pick, found that the more comprehensive the network became, the more people wished to explore and enjoy their city.

Pennsylvania Station, New York

Of New York's Pennsylvania Station, the architectural historian Vincent Scully said, 'One entered the city like a god. Now one scuttles in like a sewer rat.' Its original design (1910) called to mind the Baths of Caracalla in ancient Rome; demolished, shamefully, in 1963, its grim successor was built underground.

Venice waterways

A city on water, Venice runs an efficient around-the-clock public transport system based on river buses – *vaporetti*, or 'little steamers' – ploughing their away along principal canals and further out to the Lido and the small islands of the lagoon. Here is a city largely innocent of cars.

Cultural Buildings

As towns and cities have grown, they have often chosen to champion the arts in general, mostly perhaps as matter of prestige as well as their own local culture. The most outgoing have also wanted to display the exotic cultures that they have encountered through trade or conquest. From the 19th century onwards, grand museums, opera houses and civic art galleries rose loftily among traditional music halls, assembly rooms and pleasure gardens. By the 21st century, towns and cities vied with one another to shape the most extravagant cultural buildings.

Sydney Opera House
Sydney Opera House (1957–73) occupies a prominent position on the city's waterfront. A daring design, by the Danish architect Jorn Utzon, and ambitious structure, with its great wave or beak-like roofs, it caught the imagination of cities worldwide, while helping to change the outback image of Australia itself.

Teatro Olimpico, Vicenza

Vicenza's Teatro Olimpico (1580–85) is both a 16th-century re-imagining of an ideal ancient Roman theatre and an object lesson in urban design. Created by Andrea Palladio, its *trompe l'oeil* stage set was realised by Vincenzo Scamozzi. Here, imaginary city streets radiate from a piazza along seemingly infinite urban vistas.

Old Library of Trinity College Dublin

No worthwhile city or town is without a library. Here, the knowledge and intellectual quest of the urban mind are contained and celebrated in distinctive architectural surroundings. Few are finer than the Old Library (1712–32) of Trinity College Dublin, its high stacks interspersed with bust of great thinkers and writers.

The Louvre, Paris

The Louvre, formerly a royal palace, occupies a huge swathe of central Paris. A public art gallery following the French Revolution of 1789, it continues to expand. In 1989, a new entrance was created through a glass pyramid designed by I. M. Pei, evoking 18th-century explorations of ancient Egypt.

Museum of the Revolution, Havana

A city's culture is inevitably bound up in its history. The Museum of the Revolution, Havana, celebrates the victory of Fidel Castro's rebels over the Battista dictatorship, its home the former presidential palace, a Baroque confection of 1920 decorated by Tiffany of New York, and since 1959 with tanks and blood-soaked clothing.

Pleasure

Baths of Caracalla
A colossal leisure centre, the Baths of Caracalla (212–16) were open to people of all classes. Under 33-m (108-ft) high vaulted ceilings, Romans enjoyed cold, hot and warm baths, an open-air swimming pool and a gym. One side of the complex was given over to shops, but there were libraries too.

Cities shaped what had been tribal dances into balls and folk songs into opera. And, yet, for all their nominally civilising aspects, they also offered new opportunities for the pursuit of hedonistic pleasure. In the city, strangers and different cultures could meet as never before, sparking new forms of adventurous and even intoxicating delight, whether high-spirited dance halls, music dives, illicit shebeens, Turkish baths or assignations in public parks, along with streets and alleyways of unbridled seduction.

Vauxhall Pleasure Gardens, London
From 1785, London's Vauxhall Pleasure Gardens set along the banks of the Thames was one of the world's first major urban adventures in mass catering and mass entertainment. Garbed in flamboyant Rococo architecture, it was a visual delight and hugely popular, if a little too decadent for puritanical minds.

Las Vegas
Las Vegas – an oasis in the deserts of Nevada – styles itself as 'The Entertainment Capital of the World'. A resort city dedicated to gambling and nightlife, it is characterised by mesmeric neon signs and streets lined with eye-boggling hotels, one in shape of a giant Egyptian pyramid.

Whisky a Go Go, Los Angeles
Music clubs and discotheques are ways cities let off steam at night. Like the Whisky a Go Go on West Hollywood's Sunset Boulevard, opened in 1964, they are also places where new fads, dances – 'go go' – and music are created and made famous. For a spell, the Doors were the house band here.

De Wallen, Amsterdam
Married men and priests were banned from the medieval lanes of Amsterdam's harbour front. Sin confronted them at every nook and corner. Today, De Wallen – the city's Red Light District – is a tourist attraction, boasting a sex museum as well as hundreds of prostitutes beckoning from red-lit windows.

Bread & Circuses

Fear of the mob, of riots and revolution, required determined measures by rulers as cities grew to the size of ancient Rome, its population rising to around 1.25 million in the 3rd century CE. One measure was force – the point of a sword – yet there was a more subtle option: feeding citizens, entertaining them and thus diverting them from sedition and insurrection. Formalised and commercialised today, the echoes of this Roman 'Bread and Circuses' policy, identified and satirised by the poet Juvenal in *c.*100 BCE, haunt sports stadia, cinemas and shopping malls.

The Colosseum, Rome
The Colosseum remains the world's largest amphitheatre. Built between 70 and 80 CE, this concrete and stone colossus could seat up to 80,000 people, who came here to revel in gladiator fights, mock sea battles, executions and the slaughtering of wild animals. It was rather like 3-D cinema, with real blood.

Maracanã stadium, Rio de Janeiro

From the late 19th century, city authorities saw organised football as a way of entertaining and diverting factory workers at weekends. Rio de Janeiro's huge Maracanã stadium – a temple of football – has also been used for rock concerts. Pope John Paul II celebrated Mass here in 1980.

Impero cinema, Asmara

Painted imperial purple, the Impero cinema, Asmara (1937), designed by the young Italian architect Mario Messina, was built to celebrate Mussolini's conquest of Ethiopia and the birth of a short-lived new Roman Empire. Despite this, it continues to entertain Asmara's film fans.

Cornwall Centre, Regina

A Roman-style Corinthian portico takes centre stage in the atrium of the Cornwall Centre, a shopping mall in Regina, Saskatchewan. This seems appropriate as shopping malls are descendants of ancient Rome's ambitious covered markets and, like sports stadia, contain weekend crowds.

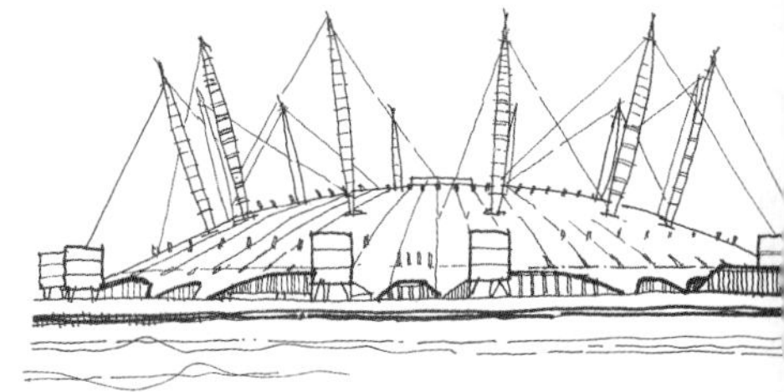

Millennium Dome, London

A lightweight Colosseum for the end of the 20th century, the Millennium Dome on London's north Greenwich peninsula, was designed by the Richard Rogers Partnership for the Millennium Experience, an exhibition promoted by Britain's New Labour government. It is now a music venue.

Food

Covered market, Rotterdam
Rotterdam's new covered market is a colourful and audacious design by MVRDV architects, embracing food and flower stalls, fashion boutiques, apartments, studios and offices. It even includes a cookery school for hurried local people challenged by what to do with real, fresh food.

By their very scale, towns and cities demanded copious amounts of food. And, yet, because there was little room or desire for farms within city walls, food was imported from the countryside beyond and distributed through markets that were housed in bigger and ever more expressive buildings. While supplying a wider population, these markets became celebrations of food, encouraging cooks and chefs. With the emergence of supermarkets, it seemed as if the civic market would disappear. It has not: freshly baked, it flourishes.

Market cross, Chichester
Market crosses were a familiar sight in medieval European towns. This is where farmers, merchants and entertainers gathered to sell their wares. Chichester's elaborate late-15th-century market cross cannot be missed: it stands at the intersection of the West Sussex town's four principal streets.

Les Halles, Paris
Les Halles was the 'belly of Paris', an immense food market that reached its zenith in the 19th century, housed in iron and glass halls designed by Victor Baltard. The market was moved to the suburbs in 1971, the old halls demolished and replaced by a shopping mall.

Al-Madina Souq, Aleppo
The most magnificent covered markets are those of the Middle East. The Al-Madina Souq in the heart of Aleppo, its structure dating back to at least 1450, has been badly damaged in the Syrian civil war. A place of sunlight, silk, spices and shadows, it boasted 13 km (8 miles) of covered streets.

Mercado Central, Valencia
Valencia's Mercado Central (1928) is a work of civic art, the food it offers as delicious as the enveloping architecture. Designed by the Catalan architects Francisco Guardia and Alejandro Soler with spectacular domes, colourful ceramics, mosaics and stained glass, it boasts a thousand stalls groaning with glorious food.

Food

Gare de Lyon restaurant, Paris
Railways spelt speed, but not fast food in Paris. Opened, by the French president, in 1901, the buffet of Gare de Lyon is one of the city's most opulent restaurants. Cuisine is served under cherubic gilt ceilings, alongside spectacular paintings and within a couple of minutes of Europe's fastest trains.

From a bare necessity to a culinary delight, the way food is eaten in public has changed as towns and cities have aged. Restaurants of a kind have existed since ancient times. To date, 158 *thermopolia*, or cafe-bars, have been uncovered among the ruins of Pompeii. The modern restaurant was cooked up in Paris in the mid-18th century. With a decline in regular meal times, city streets today abound in cafes, fast-food joints and stalls peddling drinks and snacks. Food tourism, nurtured in recent decades, has seen city restaurants rivalling long-established visitor attractions.

El-Fishawi cafe, Khan el-Khalili
Along with food, tea, coffee and tobacco are staples of venerable hubbly bubbly cafes (*ahwas*) in Middle Eastern souqs. One of the oldest is El-Fishawi in the 14th-century Khan el-Khalili market, a haunt of flickering lamps, antique wooden screens, copper tabletops and sweet-scented smoke.

Chop house, London
Chop houses were common in 18th- and 19th-century London. Like coffee houses, these public dining rooms were popular meeting places. They also provided an essential service in a city where it was easier to eat out than to attempt to cook in cramped conditions at home.

Les Deux Magots restaurant, Paris
Cafes are more than places to drink and smoke. They are places to exchange ideas as well as gossip. Les Deux Magots in Saint Germain-des-Prés is a Parisian institution, opened in 1884, and famous for those, like Simone de Beauvoir and Jean-Paul Sartre, who have thought here deeply.

Post Office Tower restaurant, London
From the windows of the revolving 'Top of the Tower' restaurant, perched high on the Post Office Tower (BT Tower today), a telecommunications marvel opened in 1964, it was once possible to look over and study London in its entirety while eating a gourmet French meal.

Parks

Parc Güell, Barcelona
The English Garden City movement encouraged Eusebi Güell to employ the Catalan architect Antoni Gaudí to design a new housing development in parkland overlooking Barcelona. The housing scheme failed, but Parc Güell developed into a delightful, almost surreal public space, a World Heritage site today.

If food markets are the bellies of cities, parks are their lungs. Ancient cities are known mostly as ruins in bare landscapes. It is easy to forget that many were beautifully and imaginatively planted. Great public parks came much later when towns and cities cried out for green space as populations soared during the Industrial Revolution. Some were former royal hunting grounds, others were entirely new creations designed for recreation and sporting tearooms and drinking fountains, ornamental lakes and play areas.

Namba Parks, Osaka
Roof gardens have been a feature of 20th-century city buildings, but perhaps the serpentine Namba Parks in Osaka, Japan (Jon Jerde, 2003), are something altogether new. Positioned on the roof of a skyscraper and adjoining shopping mall, complete with streams, ponds and waterfalls, they set a green precedent for the high-rise city.

Hanging Gardens of Babylon
One of the Seven Wonders of the Ancient World, the legendary Hanging Gardens of Babylon are said to have been laid out in stepped terraces by King Nebuchadnezzar II for his wife, Queen Amytis, who missed the lush valleys and hills of her homeland.

Botanic Gardens, Glasgow
Created originally to serve the scientific needs of Glasgow University in the early 19th century, the city's Botanic Gardens became a much-loved public park, complete with glasshouses and exotic trees, in the West End of what was once one of the world's most industrial cities.

Englischer Garten, Munich
Designed by Benjamin Thompson, a British-born American physicist and inventor, for the Elector of Hanover, and opened in 1792, Munich's expansive Englischer Garten, influenced by the English landscape gardener Capability Brown, brought the outlying countryside into the heart of the Bavarian city.

Skylines

The Blitz, London
The image of the dome of London's St Paul's Cathedral, serene amid the fire and carnage of the Blitz of 1940, expressed the spirit of a great city that was to defy the might of Nazi Germany and its attack on reason, free speech and liberty.

A city's skyline is its public face, expressing its identity, character and ambition. While temples have long soared above rooftops, from the late 19th-century skyscrapers raced up above them to proclaim the power of new forms of highly energised and technologically backed commerce. In the 21st century, the faces of age-old cities have been lifted so much that some have become almost unrecognisable. Some towns and cities prosper without skyscrapers, although these are often found on their fringes.

Liverpool

Immigration of Catholics on a large scale from Ireland to Liverpool from the mid-19th century put pressure on the church to build. From 1967, its space-capsule-like Metropolitan cathedral served as a welcome foil on the city's skyline to its magnificent if bombastic Neo-Gothic Church of England partner.

Chicago

From the shores of Lake Chicago, the 'Windy City' rises in confident, muscular fashion. The Midwest city looks every inch what it is: a powerful mercantile and industrial city that has invested its riches in bravura architecture including some of the most memorable of all skyscrapers.

Dubai

Dubai shot up from the desert sands along the Persian Gulf in the proverbial blink of an eye after oil was discovered here in 1966. A global trading city today, Dubai boasts a forest of skyscrapers including the Burj Khalifa, designed by Adrian Smith of SOM – as of 2015 the world's tallest building.

Salzburg

Salzburg's enchanting skyline of medieval spires, green copper domes, Baroque palaces, fortifications and romantic rooftops conjures the world of Mozart as well as that of *The Sound of Music*. This lovely Alpine ensemble makes the Austrian city a World Heritage Site today.

Bohemian Districts

Le Marais, Paris
Once an area of grand, aristocratic houses, the Marais fell from favour and by the 1950s was a poor, working-class district of Paris. Because its streets and buildings remained undeveloped, it became a haven of small bars, restaurants, shops and galleries, protected by conservation laws and becoming extremely fashionable.

Cities draw in successive waves of immigrants, from their own countries and from abroad. They also attract those for whom life in small towns and the countryside is far too limiting. The combination of these two movements has nurtured areas of cities where exotic attractions – food, music, languages, literature, fashions – meet those looking for new experiences and ways of life free from censorship and small-mindedness. The result is Latin Quarters and other bohemian streets where cities let their hair down.

Latin Quarter, New Orleans

The heart of New Orleans is one big Latin Quarter – hardly surprising given this Louisiana city's rich heritage. Founded by a French trading company in 1718, it was part of the Spanish Empire from 1763 and French again from 1801 before Napoleon sold it to the United States in 1803.

Soho, London

A grid of low-lying 18th-century streets, Soho is a distinctly lively district in the very heart of London's West End. Its streets buzz with bars, theatres, clubs and the remnants of a sex industry that once brought the dirty raincoat brigade and tourists here in concupiscent droves.

Greenwich Village, New York

A victim of rising property values, Greenwich Village is no longer the bohemia that it was throughout the 20th century, when this Lower Manhattan quarter bred jazz, beatniks, folk-rock, avant-garde artists and, as early as 1938, the first interracial nightclub – Café Society – in the United States.

Old Quebec

Quebec's old town is a wonder: a walled stone city in North America. Its cobbled streets bustle with university students and are home to fashionable bistros, galleries and nightlife. Latin Quarters thrive in dense, old neighbourhoods like this, but they are always in danger of being over-restored and gentrified.

Ghettoes

Venice *sestiere*

Venice gave cities around the world the name 'ghetto'. The Venice ghetto dates from 1516, a *sestiere* (divided area) of the city where Jews had to live. Intense settlement led to eight-storey housing blocks, giving the ghetto a distinct architectural character. Its synagogues and kosher restaurants survive to this day.

Despite their reputation as places of grim confinement within cities, the history of ghettos is complex. From 1084, Jews were encouraged to settle in Speyer, a city of the Holy Roman Empire, and to live and conduct their business, notably money lending, in a safe area designed to protect them. Equally, the Shanghai Ghetto of the 1940s witnessed the survival of thousands of German and other Jews during the Japanese occupation. The Japanese refused to turn the Jews interned here over to the Germans.

South Side, Chicago

A vast area of steel mills, factories and meat-packing warehouses, Chicago's South Side drew enormous numbers of foreign immigrants from the 1840s to the 1940s along with many black slaves freed after the American Civil War. Racial segregation, poverty, gangs and crime ensued: it has taken decades to address these problems.

Southall, London

Southall, a west London suburb, attracted immigrants from the Indian subcontinent from the 1950s. There was plenty of work in new light industries, hospitals and public transport. Southall prospered, becoming a successful and attractive Indian enclave that turned the idea of the ghetto on its head.

Warsaw ghetto

Created in 1940, the infamous Warsaw ghetto was a Nazi German creation. Some 400,000 Jews were squeezed behind 3-m (10-ft) high barbed wire walls into 2.1 square km (1.3 square miles) of city streets. When those not sent to extermination camps rose up against the Germans in 1943, they and the ghetto were annihilated.

Judengasse, Frankfurt

Photographs of Frankfurt's Judengasse, a gated 16th-century street outside the medieval walls, depict a seemingly picturesque German city street of timber shops and houses. The reality was an overcrowded, locked and gated ghetto reported to be narrow, oppressive and dirty. It was destroyed in the Second World War.

Cemeteries & Monuments

Père Lachaise Cemetery, Paris
Napoleon Bonaparte decreed a new type of urban cemetery beginning with Père Lachaise in the 20th *arrondisement* of Paris, opened days after he crowned himself Emperor in 1804. Adorned with 69,000 monuments, today it resembles a densely populated city in miniature.

Parish churchyards became overcrowded as the population of major European cities expanded rapidly in the 18th century, and the need to bury the dead elsewhere grew too, not least because so many dead bodies encouraged contagious diseases such as cholera. This led to the rise of cemeteries designed as memorial parks, often of great and haunting beauty. Like heroic monuments commemorating great victories, cemeteries celebrated and preserved the memories of cities. As they age, towns and cities abound in memorials.

Arch of Constantine, Rome

Victorious generals entered Rome along the Via Triumphalis. When Constantine won a key battle in 312, a magnificent arch was raised here, reminding citizens of Rome of the greatness of their city and empire. The arch inspired European and American architects at work in 18th-century cities.

Metropolitan Sepulchre, London

In 1829, the architect Thomas Willson proposed a 94-storey pyramid on London's Primrose Hill. Egyptian style was the height of fashion, and Willson's pyramid would contain five million deceased Londoners. Its prominent position says much about the 19th-century's familiarity with death. It never happened.

Monument to the Great Fire, London

A free-standing fluted Doric column, crowned with a gilded urn of fire and designed by Christopher Wren and Robert Hooke, has stood since 1677 to recall the Great Fire of London. For many years, an inscription at its base blamed Roman Catholics, falsely, for the conflagration.

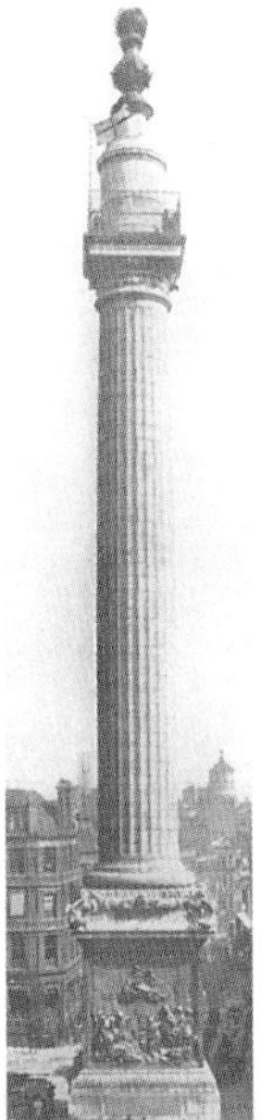

Wadi-us-Salaam cemetery, Najaf

The world's largest cemetery is Wadi-us-Salaam, a 1,400-year-old city of the dead at Najaf, Iraq. All of 10 km (6 miles) long, fighting has taken place between its countless tombs in recent years and yet rival Sunni and Shia Muslims continue to be buried here.

Media

Beyond keeping local people informed, today's newspaper and media industry, developed from printed handbills and coffee-house journals, broadcasts to the world through new forms of communication. Media organisations once sucked in and breathed out news, ideas and information gathered centrally in dedicated areas of cities such as London's Fleet Street. Electronic media has made the need for such concentration unnecessary. In the 21st century, the media operates from suburban kitchens as much as it does from dedicated streets and buildings.

The *Scotsman* building, Edinburgh
The *Scotsman* newspaper was housed throughout the 20th century in a particularly fine and romantic purpose-designed building. It occupied a singularly prominent position on the north side of Edinburgh's New Bridge connecting the Old and New Towns. The newspaper was truly at the heart of the Scottish capital.

Fleet Street, London (above)
Fleet Street, or 'The Street of Shame', was once synonymous with Britain's national newspapers. Some invested in opulent headquarters and none more so than the *Daily Express* with this Art Deco tour-de-force; it opened in 1932, when newspaper circulations ran into the several millions.

***Chicago Tribune* building (below)**
In 1922, the *Chicago Tribune* held an international competition for the design of 'the most beautiful and distinctive office building in the world'. The result was this charismatic Neo-Gothic newspaper cathedral designed by John Mead Howells and Raymond Hood. The newspaper is still very much at home here.

Apple headquarters, Cupertino (left)
Apple, the far-reaching American computer and information technology company, has been at the heart of new global media. In the second decade of the 21st century, it built a new headquarters designed by Norman Foster in the guise of a space station or giant glazed doughnut at Cupertino, California.

Patterns

Sun City, Arizona
The streets of Sun City radiate from a central core like sunbeams, appropriate perhaps for a new city laid out, from 1960, in one of the hottest, driest US states. What makes it all the more remarkable is that this is a retirement city for the over-55s.

Towns and cities may grow organically. They might be planned. However they emerge, they appear as patterns when plotted on paper or seen from the air. Some are kaleidoscopic, others as rational as a chessboard. The most enchanting, and liveable, are almost always a mixture of the two, their patterns suggesting a healthy marriage of order and exhilarating urban life. Architects, planners and rulers have often yearned and even decreed perfect, mathematical cities: few have ever really worked.

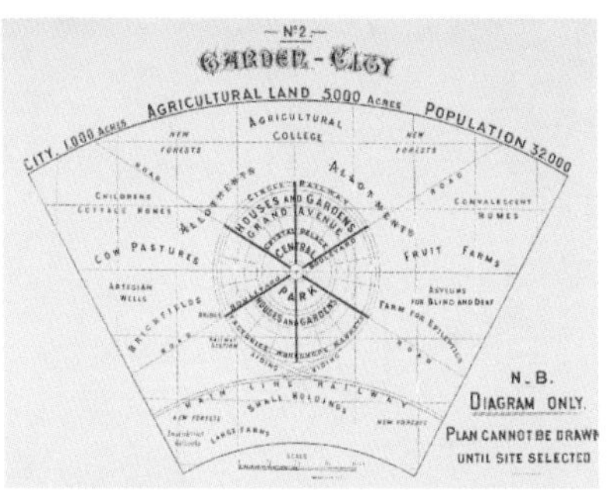

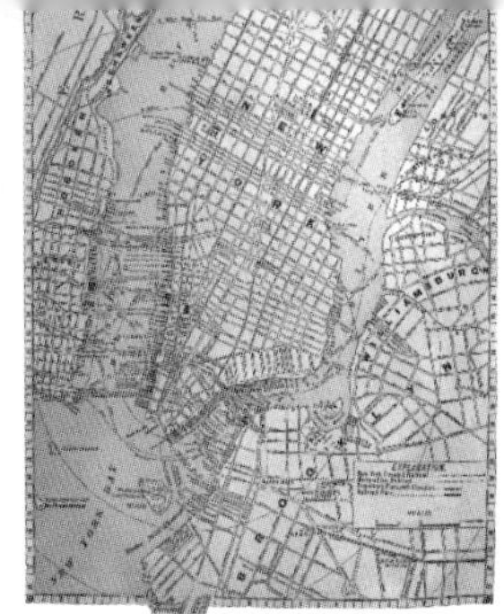

Garden cities

The Garden City was an early 20th-century attempt to offer urban settlements the best of both worlds: rational- and romantic-thinking, greenery and bustling public squares. Intriguingly, the idealised plans of Ebenezer Howard, the garden city movement's founder, appear rooted in Renaissance geometry.

Manhattan, New York

The Manhattan grid was drawn up in the early 19th century and has served New York well. Even then, the relentless nature of the grid was broken up by Nature itself with Central Park, while at either end the grid gives way to a more organic street pattern.

Palmanova

One Renaissance ideal pursued by Italian architect was that of ideal towns and cities designed and built in perfect forms. Normally these were little more than pipe dreams, but in 1593 the Venetian architect was able to realise Palmanova, a town built in the guise of a nine-pointed star.

Motorway intersections

The interweaving junctions, flyovers, flyunders and main carriageways of urban motorway intersections can be seen as ideal representations of the car-based city. Rooted in speed, they are the antithesis of an urban life measured, planned, designed, built and lived in by humans.

PART TWO City Types & Styles

Introduction

In Italo Calvino's enchanting novel *Invisible Cities* (1972), Marco Polo describes a litany of fantastical cities drawn from across an improbably exotic Mongolian empire to Kublai Khan. Eventually, the emperor realises that Polo has been speaking only of the traveller's home city, Venice, demonstrating that a marvel of such urban sorcery can be looked at and described kaleidoscopically.

Invisible Cities is a lovely conceit. And, yet, just as Calvino's narrator sees a universe in his mind's-eye evocation of Venice, so towns and cities around the world are astonishingly rich in variety and character. While they may share certain key elements, like plants and animals they have adopted a multiplicity of forms over thousands of years.

Cities have adapted to different landscapes and served distinctive purposes – ports, fortresses, financial centres – although in the era of 21st-century globalisation, they, as Calvino warned in his novel, are beginning to share a common identity as old crafts and industries give way to international retail and service industries that know no geographical boundaries and share forms of increasingly placeless, and soulless, architecture.

The city contained
Venice remains one of the world's most unexpected, intriguing and beautiful cities, proving how a city can be constructed on water and along canals and yet thrive. From the Middle Ages, it became one of the most glorious and wealthiest cities of all.

Despite this recent phenomenon, the variety of towns and cities worldwide remains as rich as the pages of an illustrated encyclopedia. At a glance, their streets and skylines tell stories of urban development over the millennia. The rise and fall of regimes and empires, from Sasanian to Soviet, can be read and decoded on entering a city for the first time, while, of course, there are cities that have all but vanished in desert sands, along dried-up river valleys and even in high mountains.

In this sense, towns and cities can be thought of as organisms that grow, mature and, for whatever reason – war, disease, climate change, complete mysteries – decline, return to nature and even vanish from sight.

The city unleashed
'The West's Most Western Town', Scottsdale, Arizona has grown rapidly from its foundation in the 1890s. Native Americans irrigated this arid landscape with canals centuries ago, and today Scottsdale, popular with residents, stretches in all directions.

Introduction

Ziggurat of Ur
With their precipitous stepped pyramids, made of mud bricks, the cities of ancient Sumeria formed an artificial mountain range in what is southern Iraq today. King Ur-Nammu built the Ziggurat of Ur, once the heart of a temple and administrative complex in the 3rd millennium BCE. It has been restored several times since.

According to *The Epic of Gilgamesh*, the world's first work of great literature, 'A reed had not come forth, a tree had not been created . . . A house had not been built/A city had not been built/All the lands were sea/ Then Eridu was made.' This was very possibly the world's first city. In the Mesopotamian mind, the city and humankind rose together. Elsewhere, between the Tigris and Indus rivers, nascent civilisations and the first cities were synonymous. Although cities can be intolerant places, it is in cities that we nurtured civilisation itself.

City of Uruk
The city of Uruk founded in around 4000 BCE reached its zenith a thousand years later. Its courtyards, workshops, streets and even its temples would be familiar to us. The course of the river Euphrates has since shifted leaving Uruk abandoned in desert sands.

Catalhoyuk
The honeycomb maze of Neolithic houses at Catalhoyuk, southern Anatolia, dates from 7500 BCE. Uncovered in 1958, this was an early form of town with a population of up to ten thousand and yet, to date, archaeologists have found no signs of social hierarchy, much less a temple.

Eridu
The ancient cities of Sumeria were not built in deserts. Eridu, founded around 5500 BCE, stood on the Persian Gulf by the mouth of the Euphrates. It was a thriving port as well as sacred city, revered even after the waters flowed away and the desert engulfed the city.

Sumerian statues
Memories of the Bronze Age kings and priests who built the Sumerian cities were forgotten even in myth and legend until archaeological digs beginning in the 1840s revealed remarkable statues of these remote founders of western civilisation, of mathematics, monumental architecture, astronomy, writing and, yes, accountancy.

The Indus Valley

Mohenjo-Daro ruins
Discovered in 1922 Mohenjo-Daro (Mound of the Dead) was one of the principal cities of the Indus Valley. No one knows its original name and, today, the ruins are in danger of crumbling away. The centre of the city – the citadel – is notable for its public baths and assembly rooms.

Five million people may have lived in the Bronze Age cities of the Indus Valley at the height of Harappan civilisation, *c.*2500 BCE. Discovered in the 1860s, these large, well-planned cities of courtyard houses were characterised by comprehensive and well-ordered water supplies, and waste disposal. They show few signs of social hierarchy, although the Harappan language has yet to be deciphered. Stretching across today's Pakistan, India and Afghanistan, chronic drought is the most likely cause for the civilisation's sudden decline *c.*1700 BCE.

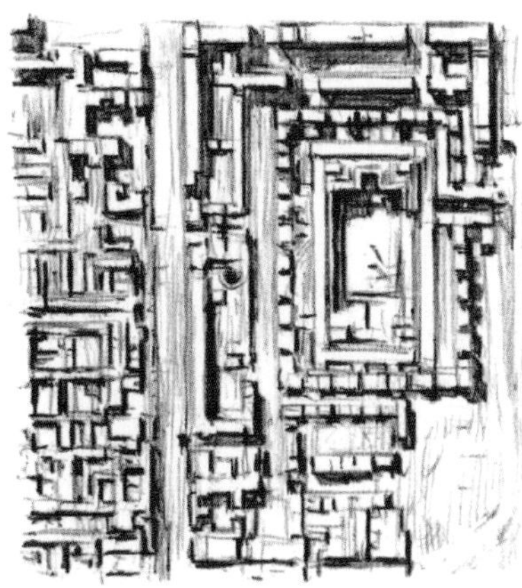

Plan of Mohenjo-Daro
Mohenjo-Daro was laid out on a gridded street plan lined with rectilinear buildings. Streets of regular houses, many with their own wells, flanked a central marketplace below the citadel. It is easy to imagine that life here may have been more civilised than in many cities until recent times.

Culture
Sculptures – many of them clay figurines and some 4,500 years old – of priests, kings, children, tradesmen and dancing girls have been discovered in the abandoned cities of the Indus Valley, offering tantalising glimpses and some insight into the life and culture of these early civilisations.

Organised society
A comprehensive network of wells, drains and sewers suggests that the Indus Valley cities were highly organised with forms of central government and administration. Not only were there public baths, but public lavatories, too, flushed, as at home, by running water. This was evidently an era of cleanliness.

Everyday life
Terracotta models and figurines depicting everyday city life, like this ox-car carrying pots, were common in the cities of the Indus Valley. They echo those discovered in contemporary Egyptian cities and offer a glimpse of life in long-dead settlements.

Ancient Egypt

The Great Pyramids of Giza

The Great Pyramids of Giza, and their attendant Sphinx, were once part of a complex city of the dead together with one of the first rigorously planned cities – complete with bakeries, breweries and a hospital – created for those who built these enigmatic monuments.

The monuments of ancient Egypt continue to haunt us, as does the history, religion, art, writing and rituals of this long-lived civilisation that owed its existence as much to the ebb and flow of the River Nile as it did to innate genius. And, yet, these aspects of life in the Egypt of the pharaohs are often seen in various forms of isolation when they were, in fact, closely tied to the life and patterns of large, ambitious and intensely busy cities. Because everyday streets and buildings of Egyptian towns and cities have long vanished, monuments dominate our distant view of them.

Temple of Apis, Memphis (right)
In 323 BCE, Alexander the Great – depicted here at the Temple of Apis – was crowned pharaoh of Egypt in Memphis. This event signalled the downfall of this once great cosmopolitan Egyptian capital, usurped by the new Mediterranean port city of Alexandria. Politics and economics determine a city's fortunes.

Temple of Seti I, Abydos (left)
The temple of Seti I at Abydos is itself laid out like a planned city, with symmetrical courtyards and halls beyond its mathematical stone facade. The temple and its gods were so important to the Egyptians that the buildings were all but synonymous with their host cities.

Temple of Karnak, Luxor (right)
The temple of Karnak, Luxor, was built by 30 pharaohs from very ancient times. Its scale and complexity are those of a city, while its mesmerising web of enclosed and open spaces, halls of columns and plays of light and shadow have much to teach us about urban design today.

Biblical Cities

Tower of Babel, Babylon
The Biblical Tower of Babel was the ambitious ziggurat – perhaps 90-m (300-ft) high – rebuilt in Babylon by King Nebuchadnezzar II (604–562 BCE) as part of a major development of the city. It commanded the skyline of Babylon, as cathedrals and skyscrapers were to do in later centuries.

The Old Testament is the story of the Jewish people, their search for a homeland and, once free of Egypt, of cities of their own. Many of the fabled Biblical cities were, in fact, no more or less than large villages or small fortified towns, while the cities that were demonised in the Old Testament – notably Babylon – were among the largest and most impressive of their time. Earthquakes may have destroyed others, like Sodom and Gomorrah.

Cuneiform script (left)
Writing emerged in Sumeria in the form of cuneiform scripts marked on clay tablets. Significantly, it was first concerned with lists of goods and foodstuffs – it was a method of recording and directing the ways cities were stocked and supplied. Writing and the rise of the city went sharpened-reed-in-hand.

Ishtar Gate, Babylon (right)
The Ishtar Gate was a part of the walls of Babylon at its height during the reign of Nebuchadnezzar II, who also commissioned the city's legendary Hanging Gardens. Sheathed in glazed blue bricks, the gate opened onto a great processional way in a city awash with colourful buildings.

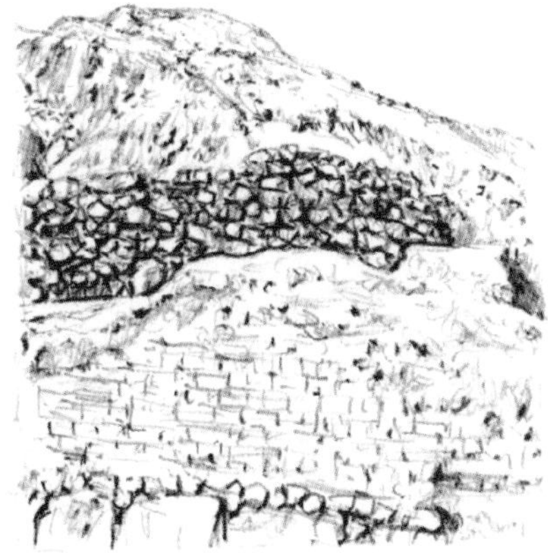

Walls of Jericho (left)
The walls of Jericho, a Neolithic settlement, collapsed centuries before Joshua's Israelite army is said to have destroyed them with the sound of its trumpets alone. The Old Testament story demonstrates, however, just how important the conquest of cities was to a people with none of its own.

Introduction

The Acropolis, Athens
The Acropolis was the citadel of ancient Athens, inhabited from the Neolithic era, but given its memorable shape and celebrated monuments – notably the Parthenon – by Pericles after the defeat of the Persians and during the ensuing 'Golden Age of Athens', between 460 and 430 BCE.

The cities of ancient Greece have inspired generations of city planners and architects for more than two millennia. With their sublime architecture, superb settings and our belief that they were the cradles of democracy along with philosophy and theatre, they have a special place in the hearts and minds of civilised people worldwide. Like the Roman cities that were to borrow so much from them, Greek cities were far livelier and messier places than scholars have often wanted us to believe.

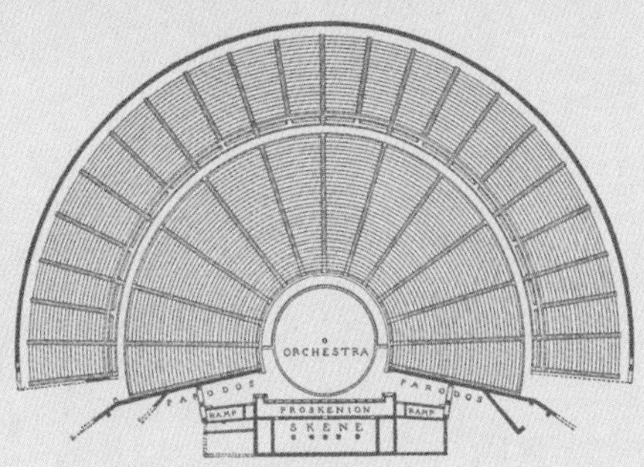

Theatre of Epidaurus (left)
Perhaps the world's most beautiful theatre, this open-air example at Epidaurus, with its perfect acoustics, magnificent views and compelling structure, was once a part of an ancient Greek healing centre, a small city enclave complete with hostels, a gymnasium and mineral-water springs. Designed by Polykleitos the Younger; built *c.*340 BCE.

Miletus city plan (right)
Miletus, a Greek city in Anatolia, was re-planned on a grid layout with straight streets leading off a central square by the architect and philosopher Hippodamus in the 5th century BCE. The first of its kind, the Miletus plan was to influence urban design for the next 2,500 years.

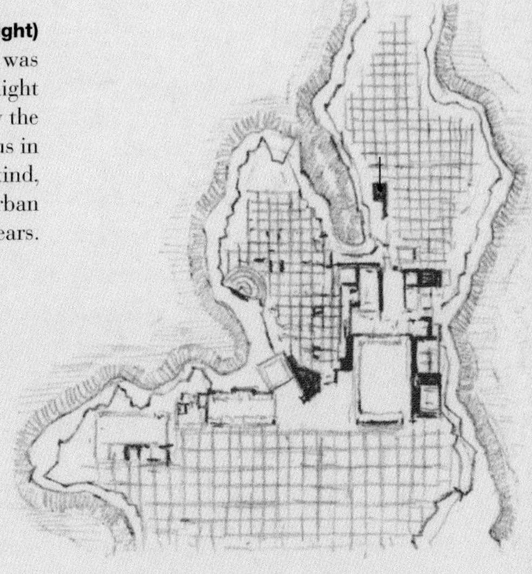

Stoa of Attalos, Athens (left)
Reconstructed in the 1950s, the Stoa of Attalos is an elegant two-storey shopping arcade, originally built *c.*150 BCE, overlooking the agora, or market square and central meeting place, of ancient Athens. Here, city trade and commerce were conducted in architecture worthy of temples and palaces.

Between Greece & Rome

The Classical world is often divided neatly between Greece and Rome. And yet, along with the influence, reach and power of these two great civilisations, important and characterful cities emerged in their bright shadows around the Mediterranean. This was the shipping route connecting Europe to Africa and Asia, linking Phoenicia to Britain, and exporting ideas about architecture, urbanism and classical civilisation over a huge swathe of the western world. Some of these cities thrived; others vanished as the power of Rome burgeoned and spread.

Carthage
The Roman senator Cato the Elder declared *Delenda est Carthago* ('Carthage must be destroyed') many times in his famous speeches. He died in 146 BCE, three years before the Romans finally destroyed this north African city, and empire, which had troubled it – and rivalled it – for so many years.

Tyre

Tyre (in Lebanon today) was a Phoenician city founded *c.*2750 BCE that thrived on trade along and even beyond the Mediterranean. Its key location also meant that, like other strategic maritime cities, it was invaded many times. Its most important archaeological sites date from the Roman era.

Alexandria

Today, Alexandria stretches 32 km (20 miles) along the Egyptian coast. Founded by Alexander the Great in 331 BCE – his architect, Dinocrates, created a magnificent gridded and colonnaded centre – the city has been invaded and badly damaged many times. Like a Phoenix it has risen time and again from the ashes.

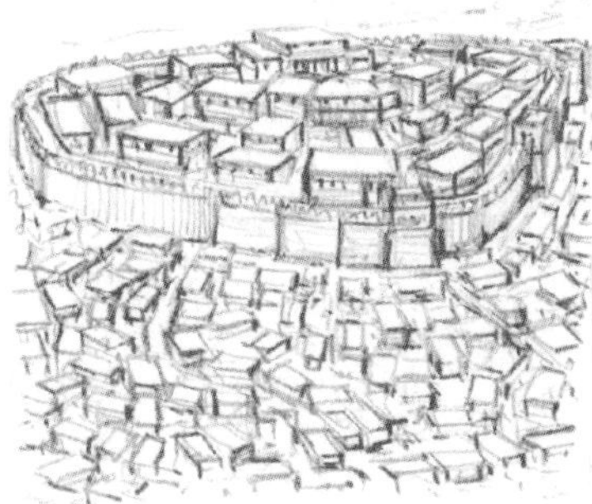

Troy

Troy was destroyed by the Greeks in *c.*1190 BCE. This ancient walled city on the coast of Anatolia (Turkey) remained the stuff of Homeric legend until its discovery in 1822, although it was not until 1988 that what had seemed little more than a fort proved to be a city.

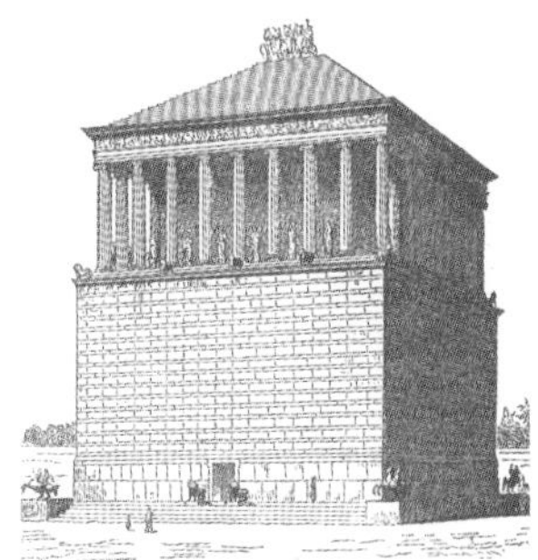

The Mausoleum of Halicarnassus

The Mausoleum of Halicarnassus (*c.*350 BCE) was one of the Seven Wonders of the Ancient World. It was the tomb of Mausolus, who transformed this island city (off the coast of modern-day Turkey) into a shining classical city of marble buildings and paved streets and squares.

Rome

The Pantheon
Emperor Hadrian rebuilt the Pantheon in 126 CE. In doing so he shaped one of the world's most magnificent and influential buildings. A temple to all the gods, the circular Pantheon is crowned with an awe-inspiring, coffered-concrete, domed vault. Today, it faces the golden arches of McDonalds.

In the chaste neo-classical halls of Mussolini's Museo della Civiltà Romana on the edge of Rome, visitors are confronted with a 1:250 scale model of ancient Rome during the reign of emperor Constantine in the early 4th century. This was a city with a population of 1.25 million and was adorned with a multitude of famous monuments and tombs, palaces and aqueducts, multi-storey blocks of flats and a maze of streets, theatres, public baths and other places of entertainment: ancient Rome was, quite simply, breathtaking.

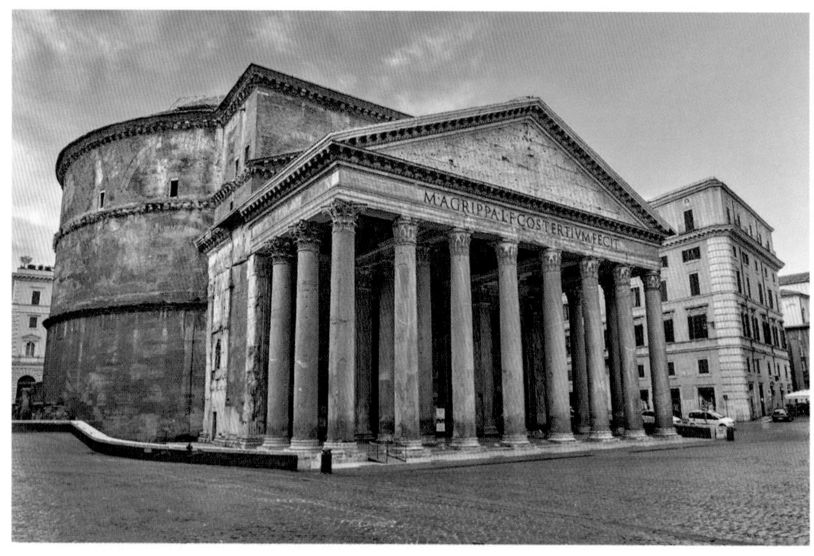

Augustus Caesar

Augustus was Rome's first emperor. Before his death in 14 CE he boasted, rhetorically, 'I found Rome a city of brick and left it a city of marble.' He did indeed initiate a huge building programme not just in Rome itself, but across the cities of its expanding empire.

Apartment blocks

Rome's ever-growing population led to the construction of high-rise concrete apartment blocks (*insulae*) – 45,000 of them in the 3rd century. Some of these were nine storeys high with the upper floors the least popular: these lacked running water and lavatories.

Baths of Caracalla

Rome's policy of 'Bread and Circuses' – keeping the populace from revolt with the offer of free food and cheap entertainment – culminated in the magnificent public baths erected by the emperor Caracalla. For a small charge, citizens had access to one of the most impressive leisure centres yet built.

The Colosseum

Opened in 80 CE, the Colosseum remains the world's largest amphitheatre. A populist gesture – it was built on the site of the gardens of the unpopular emperor Nero with spoils from the Roman sack of Jerusalem – it allowed up to 80,000 people to gawp at horrifically bloodthirsty events.

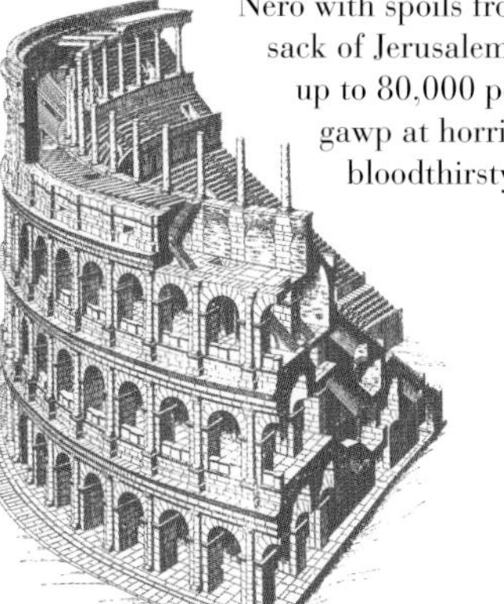

Beyond Rome

The Roman Empire was founded in 27 BCE on the back of the five-hundred-year-old Republic. It was to endure a further 450 years embracing a population of 70 million people, or one in five of the world's population. To ensure order – the *pax romana* – and a degree of commonality, cities across the empire were built or redesigned in Roman style, their plans based wherever possible on the rational grids of the Greeks. They remain an inspiration for scholars and city planners alike, although, tragically, Palmyra has been damaged by 21st-century barbarians.

Aquae Sulis (Bath)
The Romans loved bathing, especially in hot water. When they discovered the hot springs at Aquae Sulis (Bath), worshipped by the tribal Celts, they built a temple in their honour, along with the covered hot baths that, roofless today, survive as testimony to Roman urban ideals and civilisation.

Theatre at Palmyra
For centuries the oasis of Palmyra (Syria) had been a stopover for caravans crossing the Syrian Desert. When the Roman emperor Hadrian came this way in 129 CE, he rebuilt the small town into a grandiloquent Grecian city, complete with an outstanding open-air theatre leading off a long colonnaded street.

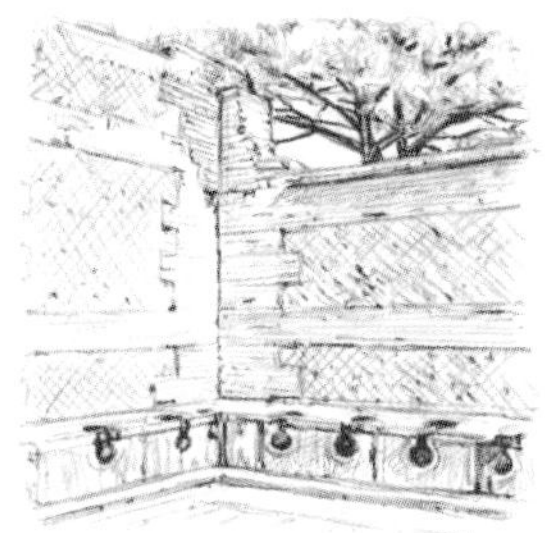

Public lavatories, Ostia
Aqueducts and all the rest aside, the Romans also gave citizens across the empire public lavatories. Many can be detected, although perhaps the best preserved are to be found in Ostia, the city port of ancient Rome itself. Often found next to temples, cleanliness was evidently next to god(s)liness.

Pont du Gard, Nîmes
The magnificent Pont du Gard near Remoulins (France) is just one part of the 50-km (30-mile) Roman aqueduct that brought fresh water from Uzes to the city of Nîmes. Built in the mid-1st century, this ambitious structure demonstrates in celebratory manner just how important fresh running water was to Roman cities.

The Library of Celsus
The Library of Celsus (125 CE), built by a Greek Roman governor of Asia, held 12,000 scrolls in its imperial heyday. It was at the heart of the Ionian city (in Turkey today) that prospered under Rome. It was destroyed by Goths, who cared little for architecture, urban planning or books.

Introduction

Forbidden City, Beijing
Ancient Chinese cities were highly structured, ordered and hierarchical. They revealed themselves through complex layers of courtyards. Beijing's Forbidden City was the former 15th-century Imperial Palace, a sequence of courtyards within courtyards with 980 buildings. It was the heart of the city itself.

The first trade mission from Rome reached China in 166 CE. Here, two of the great empires of the ancient world met. The Romans goal was Luoyang, China's oldest city, set at the confluence of the Luo and Yi rivers. Beyond the reach of Romans, however, was a vast world of Far Eastern civilisations, and thus cities, rising in splendour and isolated from the West. Ultimately, what connected them to their western siblings was trade, the lifeblood of cities worldwide.

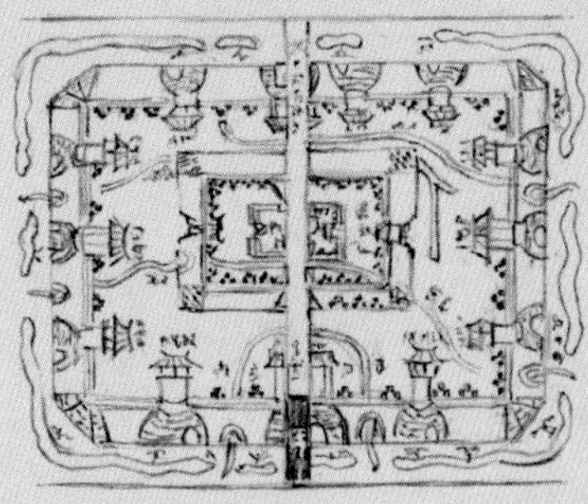

The Great Wall of China
The Great Wall of China has been built and rebuilt many times over 2,000 years. It defined and defended the first unified Chinese Empire, created in 221 BCE by Qin Shi Huang, and, importantly for the development of cities, served as a border and customs post for international trade.

Bianjing city plan
Cities like Bianjing – its plan shown here – were laid out according to precise geometries. Architecture and planning manuals issued from the beginning of the 12th century by the imperial Department of Building and Construction were used throughout China to ensure consistency in urban planning and design.

Great Wild Goose Pagoda, Xi'an
Pagodas adorned traditional Chinese cities as church towers and steeples peppered their European counterparts. First built in 652 CE, the Great Wild Goose Pagoda on the edge of Xi'an has been rebuilt many times, the victim of weather, war and earthquakes.

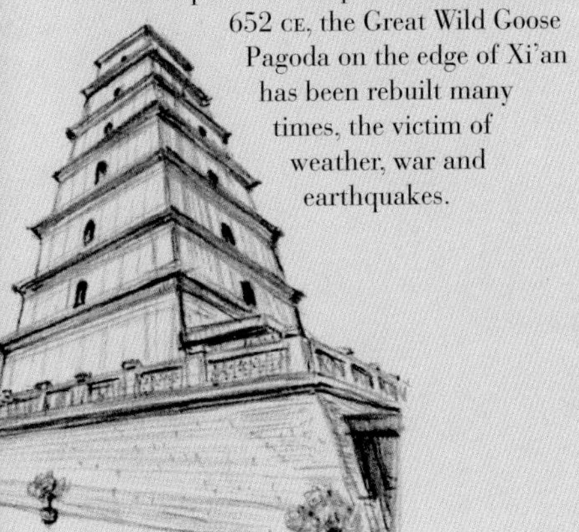

Bell Tower, Xi'an
The Bell Tower of Xi'an was built by Emperor Zhu Yuanzhang in 1384. This prominent wooden structure, set at the very centre of the city, was a symbol of imperial power and a 14th-century version of an air-raid siren, its bells rung when enemies were sighted.

Provincial Towns & Cities

Riverside buildings, Fenghuang
Fenghuang is a remarkable survival – a town built along the banks of the Tuo Jiang River, conjuring a very different China from Beijing or Shanghai. Overhanging 18th-century timber buildings on stilts, old city walls, well-trodden alleys, temples and gardens: this is an enchanting place.

The rapid economic development of China in recent decades, along with ructions caused by Chairman Mao's destructive Cultural Revolution, has transformed major historic cities out of all recognition. Increasingly, the same is true of provincial towns and cities. And yet many of the key elements of traditional Chinese urban design can be found in parts of old settlements where ancient walls, canals, courtyard housing and gardens reveal cultural ideals that have frequently been overshadowed by sensational urban sprawl.

Courtyard houses, Pingyao (left)
There are several thousand traditional courtyard houses inside the walls of Pingyao. Each is like a miniature city set within the city. Houses like these have been destroyed in much of China. Utterly delightful, some are hotels now boasting decidedly untraditional Wi-Fi and air conditioning.

The Couple's Retreat Garden, Suzhou (right)
The Couple's Retreat Garden at Suzhou (Jiangsu Province) dates from the late 19th century yet represents a long tradition of Chinese classical gardens found behind the walls of quietly grand town and city houses. Accessible by canal boat and street, it harbours 24 pavilions as well as grottoes and bridges.

Zhujiajiao (left)
Like a miniature oriental version of Venice, Zhujiajiao is a canal town near Shanghai. Founded 1,700 years ago, it prospered trading rice and cloth. It is also renowned for its fine cuisine. However, overdevelopment around its centre threatens to undermine the character and unique qualities of this special town.

Khmer Empire & South East Asia

Angkor Wat temple complex
The huge and deeply impressive Hindu-Buddhist temple complex of Angkor Wat dates from the early 12th century. Designed in the guise of a stylised mountain – the five-peaked Mount Meru is the home of Brahma, god of creation – it is surrounded by a moat and flooded with tourists today.

The Khmer Empire (802–1431), centred on today's Cambodia, grew immensely wealthy through rice production and by dint of arms. At its zenith in the 12th century, its emperors created one of the greatest cities of the age. This was Angkor Thom ('Great City'), a highly organised capital with a population of 150,000. Although the city walls, monuments, canals and temples survive, secular buildings have completely vanished. Roads, lined with guesthouses and hospitals led from here to all Khmer towns.

Khmer temples
The lotus bud crowns or capitals of Khmer temples were part of an extensive architectural vocabulary of spiritual symbols and natural carvings – especially of animals – that animated the empire's religious sites and cities. Cities were entwined with the natural world, and not apart from it.

Banten
Banten (Indonesia) is a classic example of a once important maritime city fought over by rival European powers – the Dutch triumphed in the 17th century – that has since drifted back to the status of a small fishing town in a post-colonial world. Cities do not always grow.

Borobudur Temple
From a distance the Buddhist temple of Borobudur in central Java resembles some fabled city. Close up, it proves to be a form of stepped pyramid inviting pilgrims to ascend, in the company of stone Buddhas, from the world of nearby rural villages to Nirvana or spiritual enlightenment.

Jayavarman VII
Jayavarman VII, who reigned from 1181 to 1218, was the Khmer Empire's greatest builder, a Buddhist monarch who created Angkor Thom and drew people from the countryside into centralised towns and cities. Little known until the 20th century, he is a Cambodian hero today.

Introduction

Pyramid of the Sun, Teotihuacan
Among the overwhelming buildings that dazzled the Spanish conquistadores as they marched through the Mexico Valley in 1519 was the Pyramid of the Sun at Teotihuacan. Built by an unknown civilisation *c.*100 CE, this was just one part of a monumental religious complex in a city of some 150,000 people.

'When we saw so many cities and villages built in the water and other great towns on dry land we were amazed . . . And some of our soldiers even asked whether the things that we saw were not a dream? I do not know how to describe it.' (Bernal Díaz del Castillo, *The Conquest of New Spain*). The scale, ingenuity and magnificence of American cities came as a shock to Europeans who had no idea of their existence. They were larger, cleaner and planned more rationally than those of the Spaniards who destroyed them in the name of their god.

Great Pyramid, Cholula
Teotihuacan was not alone: the great pyramid at Cholula, resembling a grassy hill today, was even bigger than the Pyramid of Sun. Cholula was a Mesoamerican city founded in the 2nd century BCE. It is said to have contained 365 temples, replaced by 50 Catholic churches by the Spanish.

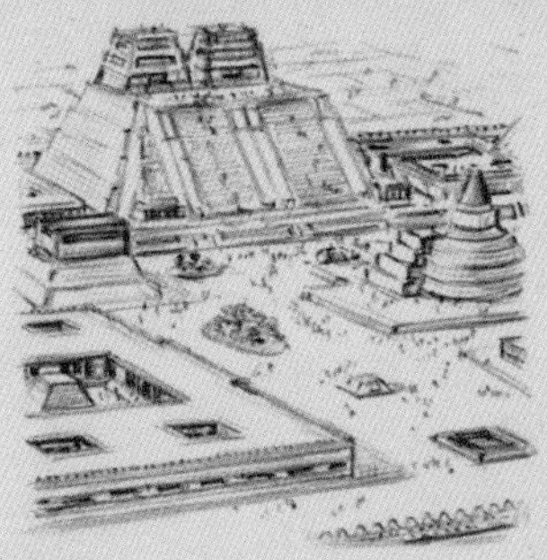

Tenochtitlan
The stunning Aztec capital Tenochtitlan was laid out on an island in the shallow Lake Texcoco from 1325. Connected to the mainland by bridged causeways, it was divided by canals, fed with water from two aqueducts and kept spotlessly clean. It was destroyed by the Spanish conquistadores in 1521.

Aztec city recreation
Masonry ball courts were built alongside city temples throughout Mesoamerica from as early as 1400 BCE. The Aztecs upheld the tradition. The game played on them – a kind of fierce volleyball – was a curious sport: winning teams were sometimes sacrificed to the gods. This was an honour.

Great Temple of Tenochtitlan
Human sacrifice was an endemic part of life in Aztec cities. At the opening ceremony of the 6th Great Temple of Tenochtitlan in 1487 some 4,000 prisoners of war had their beating hearts ripped from their ribcages and their bleeding bodies unceremoniously kicked down the temple steps.

Mayan Cities

Temple of Kukulkan, Chichen Itza
On spring and autumn solstices, the sun sends a shadow in the guise of a snake wriggling down the 365 steps of the Temple of Kukulkan, the serpent god, at Chichen Itza, one of the finest Mayan settlements. Religious ritual was the heart and soul of these enigmatic cities.

Mayans did not vanish completely as is sometimes believed. Some five million Mayans live in Guatemala today, yet their great urban civilisation comprising a network of 40 city states linked by flourishing trade routes collapsed from 900 CE. They had been famous for their temples, observatories, marketplaces, ball courts and schools. Mayans were noted mathematicians, although the Spanish who crushed the last independent Mayan town as late as 1697 destroyed most of their scholarship and writing.

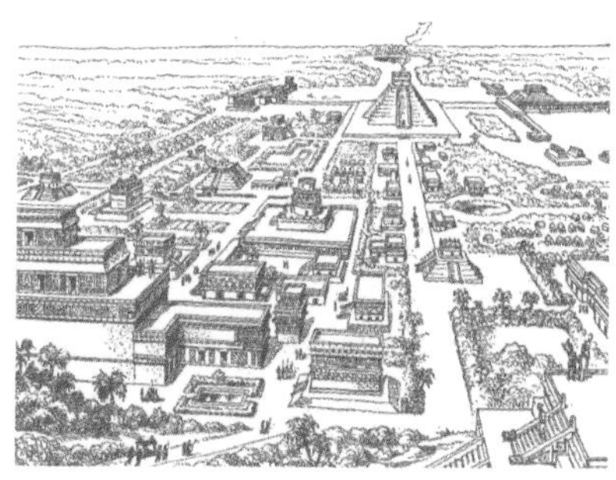

Mayan city view

The monumental core of Mayan cities contained key religious and administrative buildings as well as homes of prominent citizens. Beyond these monumental centres, cities sprawled out towards surrounding jungle. The jungle swallowed many Mayan cities, some of which are still being uncovered today.

Palenque

It seems remarkable that no more than ten per cent of the Mayan city of Palenque in southern Mexico has been uncovered. Perhaps the most captivating and legible of these cities, up to a thousand of its buildings remain hidden away in the surrounding rainforest.

Jaguar tomb, Ek Balam

The 'Jaguar tomb' at Ek Balam is a Mayan ruler's house and tomb. In the city's heyday it belonged to Ukil-Kan-Lek-Tok and in his lifetime, perhaps, it was decorated with lively sculptures set within the jaws and teeth of a stylised Jaguar: Mayan cities were laced with symbolism.

Governor's house, Uxmal

The House of the Governor at Uxmal is a powerful horizontal building decorated with a frieze of masks of the Mayan rain god Chaac. The main door of the building is aligned with the planet Venus and indeed the city's plan appears to be rooted in astronomy rather than purely earthly concerns.

Inca Cities

Machu Picchu
The Spanish were never to find much less to destroy Machu Picchu, one of the world's most thrilling cities. Located 2,400-m (8,000-ft) above sea level, the wider world only got to know of this magical place in 1911. Even today, there is no modern road to the mountain city.

The Incas emerged as an imperial power just a century before the Spanish conquistadores arrived in around 1526 with powerful weapons, treachery and virulent diseases that, combined, killed between two-thirds and 90 per cent of these Andean people. And, yet, in the brief glory years of their empire, stretching south from Peru through Chile, the Incas built a number of remarkable stone cities high in the mountains, laid out not in geometric patterns but in the shape of birds and animals.

Ollantaytambo plan

Set a thousand feet higher than Machu Picchu, Ollantaytambo was the last bastion of Inca resistance in the 16th century. Still occupied, the town is laid out on a grid plan with a large central plaza, typical of Inca cities. Handsome stone storehouses line terraced fields around the city.

Choquequirao

Until a proposed 15-minute cable car brings mass tourism here, Choquequirao can only be reached by a two-day hike up and across mountain ridges. Similar in many ways to Machu Picchu, this Inca city features glorious terraces, a levelled mountain-top plaza and a sophisticated water supply.

Sacsayhuaman

Sacsayhuaman was an Inca fortress town recreated from an ancient citadel. Its walls protected a large central plaza presumably used for religious rituals and festivals. The ruined town's lighter stones were taken down the mountain to build the Spanish colonial town of Cusco.

Huchuy Qosqo

Another two-day trek leads to Huchuy Qosqo (3,600 m/11,800 ft), an Inca town with streets of houses along high terraces overlooking the Sacred Valley. To build a town so high in the mountains – well drained and with a reliable water supply – took ingenuity, skill and what must have been sheer effort.

Introduction

House of Wisdom, Baghdad
In 762 CE, the Abbasid Caliph al-Mansur founded his new capital, Baghdad, on the banks of the Tigris. It became a seat of culture, trade and learning. Its famous House of Wisdom was the world's largest library, bringing together Islamic, Persian, Greek and Christian scholarship.

The spread of Islam between the mid-620s and 750 CE was remarkable. The new religion and its armies fanned out from Arabia and conquered lands stretching from Spain to the borders of India with the North African coast as the corridor connecting the towns and cities of this new empire. Islam brought not just a new faith but new building types and fresh forms of urban planning and design. Despite regional differences, Islamic cities were easy to recognise, their centres dominated by mosques and minarets and crowded with down-to-earth souqs.

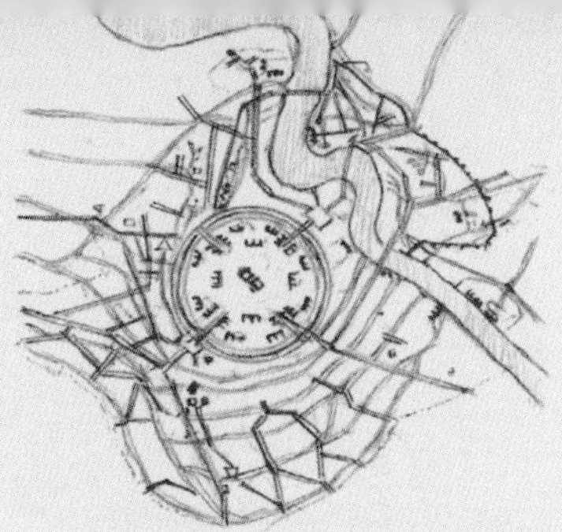

Baghdad city plan

Planned in the guise of a giant wagon wheel with radiating streets, Baghdad's was an idealised design made perfectly real. At its core was al-Mansur's palace, a place of peacocks and poetry as well as politics and religion. The city was sacked, its library destroyed, by the Mongols in 1258.

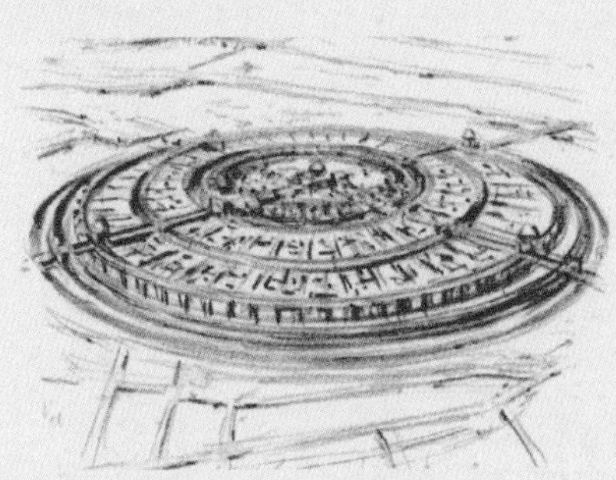

City of a million people, Baghdad

Key to the success of al-Mansur's Baghdad – by the 13th century, the world's biggest city with a population of a million – was its sophisticated water supply. When this was wrecked by the Mongols, Baghdad lost its rich supporting agriculture as well as its public baths and many fountains.

Madrasah courtyard

Madrasahs played a key role in Islamic cities. Students, scholars, scribes and scientists flocked to the new al-Mustansiriya Madrasah (1227–34). Clustered around a central courtyard, the college boasted baths and kitchens, living quarters and prayer halls as well as classrooms. Damaged in 1258, it was rebuilt and survives today.

Spiral minaret, Samarra

The exquisite 52-m (170-ft) spiral minaret of Samarra (Iraq) survived the Mongol invasion, although the main body of what was the word's largest mosque was all but destroyed; only the walls remain. Dating from 851, the mosque was commissioned by the Abbasid Caliph al-Mutawakkil, an architectural enthusiast.

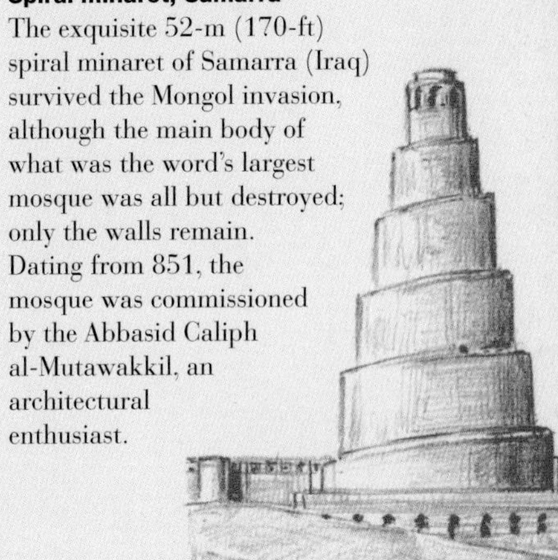

Cairo & North Africa

Ibn Tulun mosque, Cairo
The mosque of Ibn Tulun was built before the foundation of the medieval Cairo. Commissioned by Ahmed Ibn Tulun, the late-9th-century Abbasid governor of Egypt, its design is based around a giant courtyard. Chaste, even severe and militaristic, it has an elemental beauty and has survived largely unchanged.

Alexandria had long been the capital of Egypt when in 641 Arabs conquered the land of the pharaohs. After struggles between competing caliphates, the great medieval city that still exists to a remarkable extent was founded in 969. Although dynasties came and went in new Islamic wars, Cairo grew to become an immense walled city characterised by magnificent mosques and palaces along with extensive covered markets, a dramatic cemetery – the City of the Dead – and handsome merchants' houses.

Medieval Cairo skyline

The skyline of medieval Cairo is nothing short of delightful. A busy compendium of domes, minarets and other towers, it evokes still a sense of how many great medieval cities – Islamic or otherwise – must have felt like in their original heyday.

Street of the Tentmakers, Cairo

Cairo's Street of the Tentmakers survives today despite an increasing lack of interest in this age-old skill – one that connects medieval Cairo to its 7th-century Arabic routes. Some upper floors of the tentmakers' workshops have been converted into flats, yet the medieval atmosphere is still tangible.

Khan el-Khalili market, Cairo

Built and rebuilt on the site of a wilfully destroyed Fatimid mausoleum, Cairo's voluminous Khan el-Khalili market dates from 1511 and the era of the last Mamluk sultans. The magnificence of its gateways and the grandeur of its covered streets show just how important trade was to the city.

The Great Mosque of Kairouan

The Great Mosque of Kairouan (Tunisia) is a fortress-like complex concealing an intricate hypostyle prayer hall, its columns crowned with Arabic, Roman and Byzantine capitals. These evoke the invasions and conquests that led to the founding of this mosque, and city, by the Arab general Uqba ibn Nafi in 670.

Christian Cities

Hagia Sofia, Constantinople
Justinian's partially successful attempt to reunite the Roman Empire during his long reign (527–565) was accompanied by a grand building programme. The sensational basilica he built – Hagia Sofia (Divine Wisdom) – was the world's largest for a thousand years. Constantinople began to inspire a new generation of Western monarchs.

In 330, Constantine made Byzantium the capital of the Roman Empire. His 'New Rome' – Constantinople – was to flourish as a Greek-speaking Christian city. Originally its opulent paved streets, amphitheatres, palaces and baths were built using stone, marble and columns that had been shipped from the West. The city of Constantinople became a bulwark against Islamic expansion and through the Dark Ages it kept a light shining for the values of both Christianity and ancient Rome, including those of classical architecture and urban planning.

Theodosian walls, Constantinople
As a bastion of Roman and Greek civilisation into the Dark Ages, Constantinople was encircled with the last and most impressive fortified city walls of the Ancient World. Those built by Theodosius II in the 5th century when Attila the Hun was on the rampage survive largely intact today.

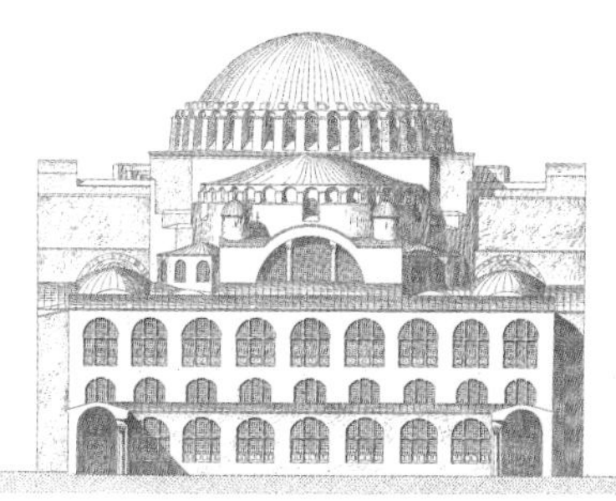

Hagia Sofia basilica, Constantinople
The scale and ingenuity of the Hagia Sofia marked a new high point in architectural design and city architecture. The great domed basilica went on to influence Christian and Muslim architecture, while the church itself became – successively – a Roman Catholic cathedral, an Ottoman mosque and a Turkish museum.

Palatine chapel, Aachen
In 800, Charlemagne was crowned first emperor of the Holy Roman Empire in Aachen (Germany). Reuniting much of Western Europe, he sought to recreate cities and buildings that lived up to his Roman predecessors. His chapel at Aachen was influenced by Byzantine design.

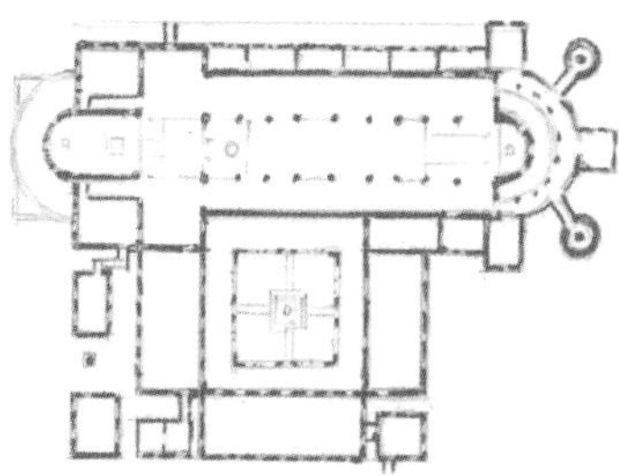

St Gall monastery plan
The Plan of St Gall is a 9th-century drawing of an ideal Benedictine monastery. It could be that of an ideal town. It was made during a synod at Aachen in the reign of Louis the Pious. It marked the revival of architectural drawing, a largely forgotten skill.

Introduction

Not all European medieval towns were cramped, crowded and unhygienic. Nor were they as charming as Robin Hood films and Victorian literary romances would have us believe. Many were characterised by informal plans, with lanes of workshops and houses winding away from market squares and following the natural contours of local landscapes. This gave these towns what we see today as a rather ad hoc, if happily picturesque, ambience. Some, like the hill towns of Tuscany, have become global treasures.

Piazza del Campo, Siena
In terms of design, the shell-shaped Piazza del Campo is one of the best-loved and most influential of all town squares. Surrounded by a wealth of warmly ambitious medieval civic buildings, it remains home to that most medieval of events, the Palio – a daredevil, bareback horse race around the square.

Medieval streets, Rothenberg (right)
Rothenberg (Bavaria) was a major town before the effects of the Thirty Years War and the Black Death laid it low in the 1630s. A lack of development preserved its medieval character. The Nazis viewed it as the 'most German of German towns' because of its unspoilt, half-timbered volkisch appearance.

Cloth Hall, Ypres (left)
The wool trade could make medieval towns extremely wealthy. The sheer scale and architectural ambition of the Cloth Hall at Ypres (Belgium), built between 1200 and 1304, show what wool could buy. Bombed wilfully by the Germans in the 1914–18 war, the Cloth Hall was rebuilt diligently between 1928 and 1967.

Place des Merciers, Dinan (right)
The narrow medieval lanes of Dinan (Britanny) lead to the town's Place des Merciers. This is not some grand classical square, but a confined triangular space centred on a well and surrounded by a happy huddle of timbered merchants' and craftsmen's houses sat under fairy-tale roofs.

European Walled Towns

Tallin

With its cluster of towers and onion domes, the skyline of Tallin (Estonia) is a delight; a pleasure reinforced by a virtually complete set of 13th- and 14th-century defensive walls and watchtowers surrounding the old city centre. What were once grim necessities are now urban treasures.

Through much of the medieval era, Europe was subject to endemic warfare. Armies marched, kingdoms rose and fell, national and regional boundaries were often fluid and towns defended themselves as best they could, surrounding themselves with walls, watchtowers and fortified gateways. Many of these were pulled down from the 18th century as the Enlightenment took hold and national boundaries began to settle and, of course, as new forms of warfare made them redundant. They remained, however, picturesque.

Dubrovnik
The independent Republic of Ragusa (Dubrovnik) maintained its much-vaunted freedom from 1328 because of its commanding location overlooking the Adriatic and the mighty walls surrounding it. Built and rebuilt over five centuries, these met their worst attacks during the bombardment of Dubrovnik by the Yugoslav People's Army in 1991–92. They endured.

Westgate, Canterbury
The centre of Canterbury is still entered by Westgate, England's largest surviving city gate. A late-14th-century replacement for a 4th-century Roman predecessor, it was built at a time when a French invasion was feared. A prison for hundreds of years, it is a museum today.

Carcassonne
The walls of Carcassonne (Languedoc-Roussillon) are world famous. Seen from a distance they lend the town the look of an untouched medieval fortress. In fact, they were very nearly demolished. After an outcry, they were restored with brio by the architect and theorist Eugène Viollet-le-Duc in the 1850s.

Freistadt
Close to the Czech border, Freistadt (Austria) stands on an important medieval salt-trade route. This, and fear of attack from neighbouring Bohemia, is the reason for its extensive 14th-century fortifications – double walls, moats, towers and gates – enclosing a well-preserved medieval centre.

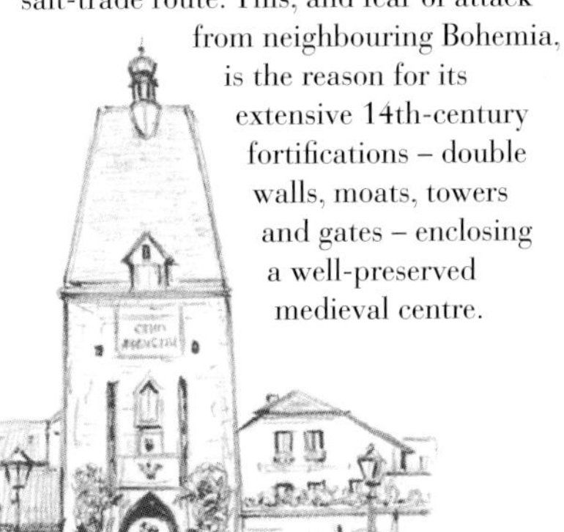

Beyond Europe

Taroudant

Taroudant is a remarkable survival. Until very recently, the town existed entirely within its beautiful set of walls built by Mohammed ash-Sheikh during the brief 'golden age' of the Saadi dynasty (1554–1659), which fought the Portuguese, held back the Ottomans and ruled Morocco. Taroudant was the dynasty's first capital.

Towns and cities around the world have sought to protect themselves with walls. Few have ever withstood prolonged and determined sieges. And, even when they have been as remote and seemingly impregnable as the Cathars' last stronghold of Montségur – a castle pressed into service as a small town – they have fallen against overwhelming odds. Today, surviving town defences are a popular tourist attraction, while new forms of walls – both concrete and electronic – protect modern city centres from terrorist attacks. And yet the more outgoing we are the less we need city walls of any kind.

Erbil

The ancient citadel of Erbil (Kurdistan) dates back to the 5th millennium BCE. Home until recently to local families, the modern city surrounds it today. In 1258, the citadel fell to the Mongols. In 2015, Erbil is a Kurdish citadel defending Muslims, Christians and Yazidis against 'Islamic State'.

Bam

Until badly damaged by an earthquake in 2003, Bam (Iran) was a remarkably intact walled town built almost entirely of adobe or sun-baked mud bricks. It was founded some time in the 3rd century, and built up over many centuries. It felt all of a piece. Reconstruction is under way.

Baku

Baku (Turkmenistan) enjoys an enviable location overlooking the Caspian Sea. The city has witnessed the comings, goings and settlement of an extraordinary diversity of people, bearing witness to many different cultures. The citadel, its walls and palace date from the 12th century. The city has grown around them.

Great Zimbabwe

Great Zimbabwe (Zimbabwe) is the largest ancient structure south of the Sahara desert. A walled Iron Age citadel or small town, its finely crafted stone walls date from between the 11th and 15th centuries. Little is known of the people who once lived and traded here.

THE BAROQUE CITY

Introduction

San Pantalon, Venice
The unfinished exterior of the 17th-century Venetian church of San Pantalon hides one of the city's greatest treasures: a staggering Baroque ceiling – oil on canvas by Gian Antonio Fumiani – depicting *The Martyrdom and Apotheosis of St Pantalon*. Its dizzying perspectives are a glorious demonstration of Baroque spatial play.

The Baroque was a profound yet highly theatrical movement in art and architecture. It was both a reaction to the cool, chaste classicism of the mid-Renaissance and a powerful tool, in the hands of the Roman Catholic Church, to propagate its faith at a time when the Protestant Reformation was changing the religious mindset and political landscape of Europe. This was the Counter Reformation, and the Baroque was its handmaiden. Along with opulent architecture, it offered new forms of urban planning.

Tempietto, Rome
Set in small courtyard of the church of San Pietro in Montorio, Rome, the domed and colonnaded Tempietto by Donato Bramante was consecrated in 1500, and yet the manner in which this noble tomb is squeezed into the confines that exaggerate its scale anticipate Baroque urban design.

Fontana dei Quattro Fiumi, Rome
Rome was the epicentre of the Baroque earthquake. The Fontana dei Quattro Fiumi (1651), sculpted by Gian Lorenzo Bernini, appears to erupt from the pavements of Piazza Navona, a market square standing on the Stadium of Diocletian transformed into an urban meeting place and architectural artwork.

Piazza of St Peter's, Rome
Bernini's elliptical Piazza of St Peter's (1656–67) is a brilliant design, representing the arms of the Mother Church embracing the multitude as they come to be blessed by the Pope. An urban and religious theatre centred on an Egyptian obelisk, it is formed of 300 travertine Doric columns.

Piazza del Popolo, Rome
The twin Baroque churches of Santa Maria dei Miracoli (1681) and Santa Maria in Montesanto (1679) served as a gateway to visitors to Rome from the Via Flaminia. This introduction to the Eternal City was improved when Giuseppe Valadier laid out the Piazza del Popolo anew in 1811–22.

Italian Peninsula

Baroque architecture and planning fanned out from Rome the length and breadth of Italy. It captured the vitality of Italian street life and imbued towns and cities with a lovable theatricality as if the very buildings and streets were alive. A thing of curves, Baroque design made classical plans more sensuous than they had been before, adding unexpected twists and turns to urban spaces. It was as if architects had become playwrights – or vice-versa – and sometimes they had. Although it was a product of ultra Roman Catholicism, Protestant cities were unable to resist the lure of the Baroque.

Chapel of the Holy Shroud, Turin
Camillo-Guarino Guarini was an architect, mathematician and Theatine priest, a part of the vanguard of the Counter-Reformation. His mind-stretching dome, soaring in tiers of complex stone geometry over the Chapel of the Holy Shroud, Turin, (1688–94), represents the art of Baroque spatial design *in excelsis*.

Piazza del Duomo, Syracuse

A great oval surrounded by Baroque palazzo, government buildings, spectacular churches and a cathedral built around a Greek temple – the ancient columns are here to see – the Piazza del Duomo, Syracuse (Sicily), is a hugely dramatic urban stage with an alluring food market attached.

Piazza del Duomo, Lecce

Rome aside, Lecce is the most determinedly Baroque Italian city. Its playful vistas, unexpected perspectives and creamy 17th-century stone buildings are a joy in themselves, but they lead ultimately to the Piazza del Duomo, a wraparound Baroque experience quite unlike any other.

Quattro Canti, Palermo

The 'Quattro Canti' is the name given to Palermo's Piazza Vigliena (1608–20) designed by Giulio Lasso. The four corners are four near-identical Baroque buildings that frame the eight-sided square. Each boasts a gushing fountain, sculptural niches, split pediments, intersecting pilasters and other gloriously theatrical devices.

Piazza San Carlo, Turin

Turin offers a procession of grand Baroque squares. The most impressive is Piazza San Carlo, laid out between 1642 and 1690 to designs by Carlo di Castellamonte, the Savoy court architect trained in Rome. Generous and shady colonnades surround the square, pedestrianised in 2004.

Baroque Beyond Italy

Royal Naval Hospital, Greenwich
The architectural vista of the Queen's House by Inigo Jones, seen through the portals of Christopher Wren's domed and colonnaded Royal Naval Hospital, Greenwich, begun in 1692, is one of the world's finest. Wren was assisted by Nicholas Hawksmoor and John Vanbrugh, architect and playwright.

Despite its intimate connection with the Papacy and Rome, the Baroque spread to Protestant England as well as to Orthodox Russia and, naturally, to Catholic countries in both Europe and throughout the Spanish and Portuguese empires. The differences between the various national and regional styles, however, were marked. No true Englishman would ever have accepted the sumptuous Baroque of Portuguese palaces and churches. Equally, few people with Latin blood in their veins would ever accept that English Baroque was the real thing.

Karlskirche, Vienna (left)
Commissioned by the Holy Roman Emperor Charles VI, Vienna's Karlskirche (1713–37) by Johann Fischer von Erlach, plays knowing games with architectural history. Its portico is that of a Greek temple; its columns are adapted from Roman models. Its twin tower, central dome and the composition as a whole are pure Baroque.

Winter Palace, St Petersburg (right)
The imposing, if colourful facade of the Winter Palace, St Petersburg, is a Baroque tour de force. The home of the Russian royal family had been reworked several times before Elizabeth (1741–62) commissioned Bartolomeo Rastrelli's truly ambitious plan described by Catherine the Great, who dismissed him, as 'whipped cream'.

Bom Jesus do Monte, Tenões (left)
The zigzag stairs leading to the chapel of Bom Jesus do Monte at Tenões (Portugal) were begun in 1722. Their style is Baroque and yet they were not just for playful show. Pilgrims and penitents make their way slowly up the theatrical stairs, praying at marked places as they go.

Introduction

Civita di Bagnoregio
In morning mists, Civita di Bagnoregio – founded by the Etruscans and set high above the Tiber – has the look of a fairy-tale town, or else of Jonathan Swift's floating island town of Laputa come down to earth. Its lifeline is a bridge too narrow for modern cars.

Its venerable hill towns are one of Italy's abiding glories. Over some 2,500 years these fortified hill settlements were transformed into some of the most picturesque towns of all. However, as the 20th century progressed, their fate became increasingly uncertain as those living here made the move downhill to more convenient, and prosperous, towns and cities on the plains. In recent years, their fortunes have revived, as tourism and weekend homes have brought new money if a less authentic way of life.

Gerfalco

Gerfalco in Maremma clusters in layers of narrow, winding streets around the walls of a former Tuscan hillside fortress that has all but vanished. Its role had been to protect a local silver mine. Individual, cement-rendered buildings here are hardly distinguished, yet taken together they form an enchanting composition.

Pietrasecca

Pietrasecca in the Abruzzo is not a tourist town, and yet the way its houses cling like limpets to the outcrop it straddles show just how determined people were to settle these defensive positions in the Italian landscape. Here, architecture, planning and geological strata are one and the same thing.

Manorola

Set on the Ligurian coast, Manorola is one of five small and closely connected fishing towns. It is distinguished not just by the bright colours of its buildings but by the way its streets, architecture and gardens are sculpted into the walls of great rocks and cliffs overlooking the sea.

Urbino's narrow streets

Hill towns are characterised by webs of narrow streets, some so steep that they are, in effect, stairways. In Urbino, these were designed for horse traffic as well as pedestrians. Today – happily – they are suitable only for the smallest cars and three-wheeled delivery vans.

Streets & Memorable Buildings

San Gimignano
Seen through squinted eyes, the skyline of San Gimignano, a Tuscan hill town, might just be mistaken for that of Manhattan. Fierce medieval family rivalries prompted ever-taller tower houses rising as high as 70 m (230 ft). Before the town was ravaged by the Black Death, there were 72 of these.

The joy of Italian hill towns lies not just in their settings but also in their rich variety. They might share certain characteristics because of the way they cling to hilltops, yet each has its particular look, its special buildings, customs and festivals. They remain an object lesson for those planning and building generic new towns around the world today: while they serve many of the same human and civic purposes each is as different as Mozzarella is from Gorgonzola. Their pattern of steep narrow streets opening into sunlit piazzas remains compelling.

Bagno Vignoni baths

The main square of Bagno Vignoni is a 16th-century pool of hot, sulphurous water fed by volcanic springs. It lends this ancient Tuscan hill town a curiously ethereal atmosphere, one poetically exploited by the Russian film director Andrei Tarkovsky in his 1983 film *Nostalghia*.

Fontebranda, Siena

Guarded by four stone lions, the 13th-century Fontebranda is a dramatic well, fountain and gateway to Siena. When John Ruskin, the great Victorian critic, last saw it there were 'fireflies everywhere in the sky and cloud, rising and falling, mixed with the lightning and more intense than the stars.' (*Praeterita*,1885–9.)

Pilgrimage to Loreto

Protected by heroic 16th-century walls, Loreto is a pilgrimage town dominated by the magnificent architecture of Donato Bramante around Piazza della Madonna. Why such magnificence in a small town? Inside the church is the 1st-century House of Mary, flown here – in legend – from Nazareth by angels.

Monster's Grove, Bomarzo

When his beloved wife died, Pier Francesco Orsini, a 16th-century soldier and arts patron, created the beguiling Monster's Grove at Bomarzo, a hill town overlooking the Tiber. With its abstracted Mannerist architecture and grotesque sculpture, this was designed to astonish visitors and, in doing so, to 'set their hearts free'.

Introduction

Some creation myths have humankind born in gardens, others in cities. Because cities are synonymous with civilisation, authors of Bronze Age religious texts, wittingly or not, were tempted often to equate the rise of humanity with the rise of urbanity and of the city itself. This encouraged the idea of the 'City of God', a place at the heart of Heaven, and a spiritual guide showing how to order life on earth in sacred streets and hallowed squares.

Christ the Redeemer, Rio de Janeiro
Since 1931, a 30-m (98-ft) concrete and soapstone sculpture of Christ the Redeemer has overlooked Rio de Janeiro from the 700-m (2,297-ft) peak of Corcovado. The statue says 'Rio' as surely as the Eiffel Tower says 'Paris'. More than this, though, it imprints Christianity, and God, on the teeming city below.

Jerusalem

The world's three great monotheistic religions – Judaism, Christianity and Islam – meet in the heart of Jerusalem: the Western Wall of the Jews, the Church of the Holy Sepulchre and the Temple of the Dome of the Rock sit close together on the site of Solomon's and Herod's temples.

God's own city

For centuries, Jerusalem – God's own city – was depicted as being at the very centre of the world. In 1581, the German protestant pastor and theologian Heinrich Bünting published a map of the world in the guise of a cloverleaf with Jerusalem at its heart, binding Europe, Africa and Asia together.

Chartres Cathedral

Pilgrims have walked in ever-decreasing circles around the 13th-century labyrinth set into the floor of Chartres Cathedral for the past 800 years. Quite why they do so is a mystery, although one suggestion is that the route of the labyrinth leads to the New Jerusalem.

Golden Temple, Amritsar

Surrounded by the Pool of Nectar of Immortality, the Golden Temple of the Sikhs was built between 1588 and 1604, shortly after the founding of the holy city of Amritsar (India). The four doors of the temple, facing the cardinal points of the compass, invite the world to this sacred centre.

Great Religious Cities

Mecca
Mecca, the birthplace of Mohammed, was a small spice-trade settlement until the rise of Islam. What it had that was special, even before Mohammed, was the Kaaba, a sacred shrine in the form of a stone cube that has long been thought of as a gateway between heaven and earth.

Many, even most, of the world's great towns and cities have been founded on trade. Some, though, have emerged on the back of religious fervour, while others have been transformed by the power of new religions. When religious and political power have been more or less synonymous, the streets and skylines of towns and cities have blossomed with fronds and clusters of domes, towers and spires proclaiming in no uncertain architectural terms the dominance of gods and God.

Pagan (left)

For a period of 250 years at the height of the Burmese Kingdom of Pagan, some ten thousand Buddhist stupas, pagodas, temples and monasteries were built in the city known as Bagan today. The medieval city, a centre of international scholarship, was fuelled by religion. It fell with Mongol invasions.

Vatican City (right)

St Peter, a Galilean fisherman who went on to Rome, where he became the first Pope, is buried under the vast and opulent basilica that bears his name. Its heroic Renaissance dome has dominated the skyline of the Vatican City and Rome itself since its completion in 1590.

Salt Lake City (left)

No one had settled permanently in the arid valley where Salt Lake City stands today until Brigham Young and his Mormon followers came here in 1847. They began by building a mountainous temple. Since then, mining, railways and highways have made Salt Lake City the 'Crossroads of the West'.

Religious Towns & Cities

Santiago de Compostela
Medieval pilgrim badges in the shape of scallop shells have been found throughout Europe, demonstrating how religious devotees came far and wide to Santiago de Compostela, a Galician town that thrived after its reconquest from the Moors and, miraculously, received the body of St James's, one of Christ's 12 apostles.

The variety of religious experience has shaped towns and cities in a multiplicity of configurations and purposes. In many towns, religious and secular lives have long gone hand-in-hand with places of worship fronting and even rising directly above busy market squares. In Istanbul, the exquisite Rüstem Pasha Mosque designed by Sinan, the justly celebrated 16th-century Ottoman court architect, is found on top of the local spice market, accessed by all-but-secret stairs set between market stalls. In other cities votive shrines can be found on street corners, a reminder of belief beyond the everyday.

Varanasi ghat baths

The maze of narrow streets that characterise Varanasi (India) open up at many points to ghats (steps leading to water) lining the River Ganges. Here, Hindu pilgrims mix with tourists as they bathe, meditate and light funeral pyres for the deceased. Varanasi is a city where life, death and rebirth mingle intimately.

Khajuraho

The 10th- and 11th-century Kama Sutra sculptures of the Hindu and Jain temples of Khajuraho (India) have made this religious complex world famous since its rediscovery in 1838. The town itself seems almost an afterthought. Desecrated in the era of Muslim rule, 22 of the original 85 temples survive.

The Golden Temple, Kyoto

The Golden Temple at Kyoto (Japan) was built as Shogun's retirement villa. When he died in 1408, it became a Zen temple. It has been lovingly rebuilt many times since, after fires, wars and earthquakes. It is one of 1,600 temples in and around Kyoto, a city of quiet religion.

Great Mosque, Djenne

The glorious mud Great Mosque of Djenne (Mali), successor to much earlier structures, dates from 1907. The annual festival when the mosque – facing the market square – is re-plastered has long involved many young Djenne men. Sadly, they are leaving for life in modern towns and cities.

Introduction

New York
Tides brought new people to New York. 'Give me your tired, your poor/Your huddled masses yearning to breathe free . . . Send them, the homeless, tempest-tost to me'. These lines, by Emma Lazarus, are from a sonnet engraved on a plaque in the base of the Statue of Liberty.

Tides are essential to so many thriving cities, both ancient and modern. Tides allow boats and ships reliable entry and egress to and from urban ports. Tides clean ports, harbours and the estuaries of rivers passing through towns and cities. Tides bring danger, too, with the threat of floods, and yet a special city like Venice seems only all the more characterful for its days of high water, when its buildings and squares are mirrored in inundated paving stones.

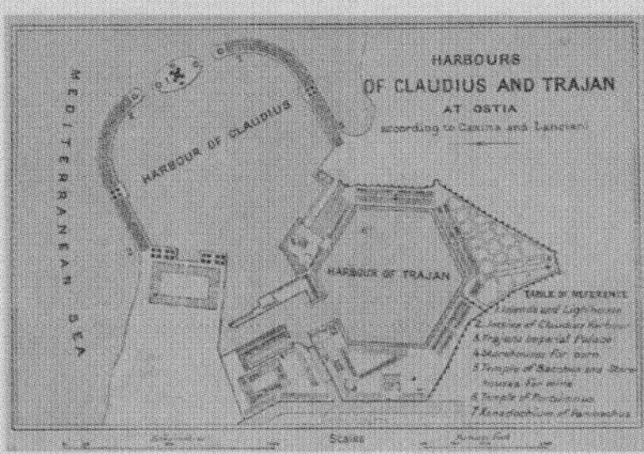

Ostia

Ostia was the first of Ancient Rome's seaports. From functional beginnings, it became a town in its own right with a population of as many as 100,000 by the 3rd century. Abandoned in the 9th century, Ostia was used as a stone quarry by the architects of Baroque Rome.

Rotterdam

Rotterdam, Europe's largest port, and Amsterdam, the centre of the 17th-century Dutch trade in spice, diamonds and money, grew to become two of the continent's most important cities through their direct links to the sea, inland waterways and, through navigational skills, the rest of the world.

Port of London

Set far from the sea, but on the tidal Thames, the Port of London connected the city to the world's oceans. At its height in the years leading up to the First World War, the Port was London's beating heart.

Felixstowe

Giant container ships bringing a surfeit of cheaply manufactured goods and gewgaws from China to an insatiable, consumer-crazy 21st-century Britain loom over Felixstowe. At heart this is a small seaside Suffolk town, yet it boasts a port big enough for vast freighters and intense global trade.

London

River Thames
London's special relationship with the sea via its tidal river – the Thames – nurtured the city's relentless commercial drive. Set 48 km (30 miles) from the English Channel, the city was largely impregnable before the age of the Zeppelin and bomber aircraft. The 18th-century painter Canaletto made it look serene.

London's roots lie in the Bronze Age; yet the city that rose to become one of the world's most powerful, and the heart of an empire that once ruled a quarter of the world's population, was founded by the Romans following the Claudian invasion of 43 CE. Burned to the ground by Boudicca and her British rebel army, the city was rebuilt and prospered. Significantly, Londinium was not the capital of Roman Britain; it was, though, the centre of imperial trade. Tidal cities have often been the world's most dynamic, outgoing and prosperous cities.

Thames Estuary

As the River Thames flowed east from London to the sea, it did more than send ships out to all four points of the compass. It also bore effluence away from the city and for centuries this stretch of the river was London's partly self-cleansing backyard, or sewer.

Tower Bridge

Tower Bridge is the gateway between what was once the industrial Thames and the commercial river coursing past the City of London. Opened in 1894, it was a masterpiece of Victorian engineering, yet it was dressed in ecclesiastical medieval Gothic garb: London's relationship with the Thames was all but religious.

Billingsgate Fish Market

In the 19th century, the City of London's Billingsgate Fish Market was the world's largest, its trade conducted from 1877 in a handsome Italianate building stretching along the Thames. In 1982, as part of a trend to move wholesale markets from city centres, Billingsgate went to the Isle of Dogs.

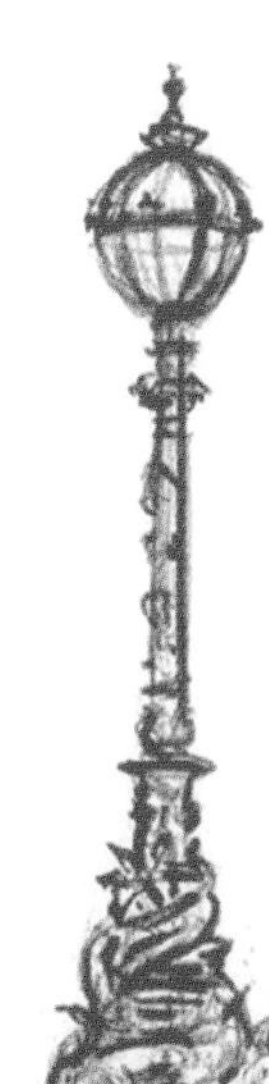

Dolphin lamps

Although looking suspiciously like sturgeon, the Dolphin lamps adorning and lighting the Victorian embankments along the Thames as it passes through central London connect the city to the sea in a direct and charming manner. Designed by the architect George Vulliamy, they appeared from 1870.

New World Transatlantic Cities of Trade

Palos de la Frontera
Columbus sailed from Palos de la Frontera, a small coastal town in Andalusia. The town was a fairly new and prosperous settlement. With the discovery of the Americas its citizens headed west to make new fortunes and Palos declined precipitately, an unexpected consequence of the rise of transatlantic towns.

In 1492, the Genoese explorer we know as Christopher Columbus sailed west across the Atlantic in search of the East Indies. His voyage took him to the Caribbean and the Americas. In later years, North America was found to be lightly populated with native 'Indians', but for Europeans it was, like South America, virgin territory, an opportunity to export old prejudices and, sometimes, to start afresh. New towns and cities were founded, becoming ever more different from their European predecessors.

Staten Island Museum
The oral archives of the Staten Island Museum hold recordings of first impressions of the United States on European emigrants. The first thing one young Irishman saw of his new home was not the Statue of Liberty, but the Neo-Gothic spire of the Woolworth Building, a symbol of democratic, get-up-and-go success.

New York skyline
The sight of ocean liners – as long as New York skyscrapers were high – berthed along the Hudson on the west side of Manhattan was not just soul-stirring, but a powerful and haunting expression of the way in which this great maritime city was the product of transatlantic trade and European culture.

World Trade Center
Destroyed by fanatical terrorists in September 2001, the twin towers of the World Trade Center anchored New York's financial district. They were a dramatic, high-rise symbol of how New York, a city of immense trade and energy, reached out to business around the globe.

Public transport
Those arriving in New York and struggling through JFK airport and the tail-back ride to Manhattan ought to regret the fact that so few long-distance trains run today from Grand Central station, a magnificent Beaux Arts railroad palace dating from 1903 at the heart of Midtown Manhattan.

New World Fortified Colonial Cities

Havana
Havana, the largest and most lucrative Caribbean city was quickly fortified. Between 1590 and 1630 the Castillo del Morro, designed by the Italian military engineer Giovanni Battista Antonelli, was built to prove Spanish might. In 1762, the British took it and Havana. Spanish power was never the same again.

While North American towns and cities were often either practical affairs or designed along idealistic Enlightenment lines, their Latin America cousins were shaped by the Catholic culture and imperial ambitions of Spain and Portugal in no uncertain terms. This resulted in the destruction of entire cities created by indigenous cultures and the emergence of Iberian cities in their stead with their bravura churches, palaces, monasteries and fortresses. Over time, a colonial style of architecture and planning adapted to the climate emerged.

Plaza Vieja, Havana

The author was very nearly crushed to death in 1993 when an 18th-century corner building in Havana's Plaza Vieja (formerly Plaza Nueva) collapsed. Since restored, this handsome square first laid out in 1559 has been used for fairs, markets, bullfights, executions and grand civic parties.

Port Royal, Jamaica

Laid out on a peninsula north of Kingston Harbour, Port Royal was a fortified Spanish city founded in 1518 when the local Taino people were enslaved. Captured by the British in 1655, it was a haven for pirates before an earthquake destroyed it in 1692.

Cartegena, Colombia

The colourful streets and buildings of old Cartegena (Colombia) form a UNESCO World Heritage Site. Their opulence stems from the Caribbean port city's extensive trade in precious metals and the huge subsidies paid by Spain to keep this valuable colonial outpost free from the clutches of the Royal Navy.

Avenida de Mayo, Buenos Aires

Laid out by Juan Antonio Buschiazzo, an Italian-born architect, between 1885 and 1894, the Avenida de Mayo (Buenos Aires) is a wide, 1.5 km (1 mile) city street designed to rival the contemporary grand avenues of Madrid, Paris and Barcelona, and named after the May 1810 revolution that sparked Argentinian independence from Spain.

Baltic Cities

Palace Square, St Petersburg
After the 1812 defeat of Napoleon, Alexander I transformed St Petersburg's Palace Square into a colossal monument to the Russian victory. Beautifully coloured, ordered and heroic military buildings by Carlo Rossi, an Italian architect, among others, joined the 18th-century Winter Palace.

The Baltic Sea is bordered by Sweden, Finland, Russia, Estonia, Latvia, Lithuania, Poland, Germany and Denmark. It is natural, then, to find common ground in the design, planning and characteristics of Baltic cities. While some of these cities, however, are ancient, others emerged remarkably late – particularly from a Mediterranean perspective – not least because of a challenging climate. Here, though, are some of the most beautiful of all cities, working with extremes of heat and cold, darkness and light.

Peter the Great

Determined to extend Russia's military reach and to modernise his country, in 1703 Peter the Great founded St Petersburg, the world's most northerly city. Its construction caused the deaths of thousands of serfs and Swedish prisoners of war. Even so, Peter's episodically tragic city was well planned and extremely beautiful.

St Petersburg plan

The plan of St Petersburg incorporates radiating streets and avenues, grand squares, long and carefully framed vistas, and buildings rendered in colours that glow both in long summer days and with snow in the depth of winter. A network of canals lends the city an air of a Neo-Classical Venice.

Helsinki Cathedral

Helsinki offers one of the most memorable entries to any major city by sea. Above distinguished Neo-Classical buildings, handsome streets, avenues and squares, the pristine white Neo-Classical cathedral (1830–52) crowns this maritime scene.

Sveaborg

For 500 years Finland was ruled by Sweden. Threatened by Russia, the Swedes built Sveaborg (1748), a star-castle spanning six islands. Sophisticated military engineering was matched by elegant architecture. Sveaborg was renamed Suomenlinna after Finnish independence in 1917

Amsterdam & Copenhagen

Prinsengracht, Amsterdam
Prinsengracht is the fourth and longest of Amsterdam's principal canal streets laid out in the early 17th century. Built from west to east like the sweep of a giant windscreen wiper, according to Dutch journalist and historian Geert Mak, these residential and defensive streets shaped the city's plan and identity.

Both Holland and Denmark enjoyed a 'Golden Age' in subtly different ways in the 17th and 18th centuries. Both European mercantile powers revelled in admirable seamanship and superb ocean-going ships. These brought great wealth to Amsterdam and Copenhagen, both cities investing in subtle yet imaginative and beautifully crafted buildings and thoughtful urban planning. The elegant restraint evident in the design of both cities was partly a product of the tenets of Protestant Christianity that shaped the values of Northern Europe.

Grachten, Amsterdam (left)
Amsterdam boomed economically in the first decade of the 17th century. A decision was made to extend the city in concentric fashion. This thinking led to the famous *grachten*, an idea that took hold until after the Second World War when a less subtle geometric expansion prevailed.

Nyhavn, Copenhagen (right)
Noted for its colourful late-17th-century houses, Nyhavn (New Harbour) was long associated with crime and prostitution. Created by Christian IV of Denmark, and built by Swedish prisoners of war, this maritime district – home of Hans Christian Andersen – is a haven mostly for tourists today.

Stock Exchange, Copenhagen (left)
Built during the long reign (1588–1648) of the ambitious Christian IV, Copenhagen's Stock Exchange was a grand building chasing international finance and trade. Its crowning glory is its spire, an intertwining of four sea-serpents' tails: the Danish city looked to the wider sea for trade and prosperity.

Southern Hemisphere

Sydney Harbour
Sydney Harbour's bridge and opera house are two of the world's most famous structures. One purely functional, the other wholly cultural, together they elevated the status of Sydney. Both exude drama, urban romance and supreme constructional and engineering skills. We judge the city by them.

Following Captain James Cook's landing in Botany Bay (Australia) in 1770, the British government set up a penal colony here under the command of the insightful Captain Arthur Phillip. Eventually Sydney, as it was named, thrived. The export of British convicts to Australia ended in the early 1840s. Soon afterwards, gold was discovered and the city with, according to Captain Arthur Phillip, 'the finest harbour in the world', developed into one of the world's most dynamic and most beautifully sited cities.

Sydney business district (right)

Sydney grew to be the hub of business in the Asia-Pacific region. Its Central Business District (CBD), or 'the City', boasts a forest of skyscrapers interspersed with a wealth of cultural institutions and nightlife. For those arriving by suburban ferries or the sea today, the City is the gateway to Sydney.

Bondi Beach (left)

Sydney's relationship to the sea is more than commercial. Bondi beach is just 6.4 km (4 miles) east of the city's CBD. A public beach since 1885, it was long at the heart of a working-class and immigrant suburb. Gentrified since, in 2008 it was placed on the Australian Heritage List.

Cape Town (right)

On the same latitude as Sydney, Cape Town was settled permanently by the Dutch East India Company in 1652. Surrounded by mountains, the old city nests in a natural amphitheatre and enjoys a Californian climate. Although it has sprawled, its centre and setting remain glorious.

Far East

Pudong, Shanghai
Like a Far Eastern Manhattan, the skyline of Pudong – the East Bank of the Huangpu River flowing through Shanghai – is composed principally of skyscrapers. These are new, sprouting since Pudong was made a Special Economic Zone in 1993. Within 20 years, a quarter of Shanghai's 20-million population lived here.

Far Eastern cities facing the East China Sea and the Sea of Japan towards the seemingly infinite latitudes of the Pacific Ocean were long cut off from the Western world. The Romans established trade routes to China, but the Silk Route was long and arduous. From the 17th century onwards, Europeans sailed to China: sea routes revolutionised commerce, and politics, between East and West. When the United States and Canada encompassed west coasts of North America, eastern seaport cities grew in importance, and trade across the Pacific Ocean became a profitable concern for cities both west and east.

Trans-Siberian Railway

The arrival of the Trans-Siberian Railway in 1916 revolutionised Vladivostok. Today, 30 per cent of Russian exports travel by the 9,289-km (5,772-mile) line. Millions of emigrants from western Russia settled in Siberia and even far-flung Kamchatka. The city boasts a wealth of late-19th- and early- 20th-century architecture.

The Bund, Shanghai

Parading along the Huangpu River north of the old walled city of Shanghai, the Bund was built, initially by the British, as a centre of international banking and commerce. Its buildings are special – there is a wealth of Art Deco gems – and the street is preserved today.

Vladivostok

During the Soviet era, Vladivostok was closed to foreigners. Home of the Russian navy's Pacific fleet, it is also a major fishing and trading port. Settled by Russians in 1860, the area had been home to the Udege, a people very similar to Native Americans.

Songjiang New City

Songjiang New City is an attempt to woo middle classes from overcrowded Shanghai. Thirty kilometres (20 miles) distant, it features nine 'cities' within the new city, based on ersatz international design themes. Thames Town (Atkins, 2006) is a Hollywood England, complete with a fake fish and chip shop.

Introduction

City Hall, Stralsund
Stralsund's superb brick Gothic medieval city hall remains the seat of local government, a symbol of the mercantile might of this beautifully preserved Hanseatic island city, founded in 1234, that retains its venerable street pattern along with many of its original buildings.

The Hanseatic League was a medieval trade association of independent cities along the north coast of Europe. Emerging from Lübeck in northern Germany, it gained official stature in 1356, encompassing merchant cities as distant from one another as Novgorod and York via the Baltic coast and the North Sea. The Hanseatic League, powerful until the 17th century, was able to raise its own army, battle pirates and fight wars. It also produced magnificent mercantile buildings that are some of the glories of their age.

Lübeck plan

Famous for its marzipan and medieval-brick architecture, Lübeck was the principal city of the Hanseatic League. It, too, was an island city, well protected before the advent of modern warfare. Badly damaged by British air raids in 1942, the old city has been restored faithfully.

Bruges

When Hanseatic trade extended to Bruges, Baltic merchants discovered a city that was already home to Italian banks and the world's first bourse, or stock exchange, named after the local Van der Beurse family. Here was a medieval city enjoying a golden age in art, architecture, trade and commerce.

Gamla Stan, Stockholm

Gamla Stan, the old island city of Stockholm, dates from the 13th century. Much loved today as a tourist attraction, with its winding medieval streets and its architecture, its design was influenced considerably by northern German practice, with ideas and even craftsmen arriving on the back of Hanseatic trade.

Lübeck market square

Lübeck's medieval market square boasts an emphatic pillory. The idea of the honest merchant was matched by public humiliation for those who transgressed Hanseatic codes of practice. Adolf Hitler was punished by not being allowed to campaign in Lübeck; he retaliated by ending the city's independence.

Trading Towns

Medieval Hanseatic town
Late medieval illustrations of Hanseatic towns are not merely charming and colourful. They reveal the wealth of this league of towns, depicting merchants – directing sea trade – in fine fur hats and gowns. Religious matters and ecclesiastical buildings tend to dominate most medieval illustrations.

The Hanseatic League established outposts in coastal towns far from Lübeck. Merchants and traders took ideas about architecture and city planning with them as they sailed the north European coast, which is why it is possible to find medieval buildings, and others up until the mid-17th century, that resemble German counterparts, in towns far from the Baltic coast. Architectural ideas have travelled as much through commerce as through intellectual and artistic discourse and, although painted with a broad brushstroke, there is indeed a Hanseatic style of design. This connects Norfolk to the north German coast, a precursor to the ways in which global trade exports architecture and city plans today.

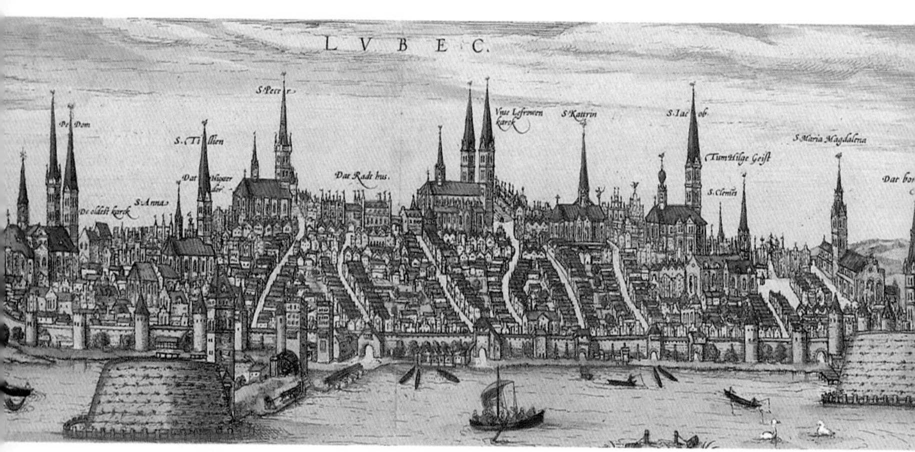

Hanseatic warehouse, King's Lynn

The last Hanseatic warehouse in England is in King's Lynn, once England's third most important port. German merchants traded herring, timber, wax, iron, pitch and grain in King's Lynn for wool, cloth and salt. By the early 15th century, the East Anglian town was famous for its German shoemakers.

Danzig/Gdansk

Danzig (German) or Gdansk (Polish) was batted backwards and forwards between German and Polish claims and armed forces over many centuries. Its strategic position on the Baltic made it vulnerable to competing interests. All but destroyed in the Second World War, it was rebuilt but largely without historic German buildings.

Hapag-Lloyd building, Hamburg

One of Hamburg's most unavoidable waterfront buildings is the Neo-Classical headquarters of the shipping line, Hapag-Lloyd. Formed in 1970 as a merger between two 19th-century companies, Hapag-Lloyd's history tells the story of a trade in people: large-scale emigration from Germany and Eastern Europe to the United States.

Riga

A key stop on the Viking trade route to Byzantium, Riga blossomed when it joined the Hanseatic League. Rich in medieval streets and buildings, Riga boomed again in the late 19th century and is renowned for Art Nouveau architecture – a restless city of trade owned by successive warring nations.

Introduction

Industrial housing
Industrial cities had an insatiable need for labour. Workers' housing sprung up rapidly, row upon row of cheapjack, unsentimental back-to-back houses seemingly cocking a snook at urbane 18th-century manners and Georgian architectural grace. They were evidence that industrial fortunes were made on the back of meanness and ragged-trousered misery.

The Industrial Revolution changed the faces of many towns and cities almost out of recognition, beginning in Britain before exporting its manifesto of machine-driven manufacturing around the globe. It engendered entirely new towns, and covered existing cities in soot and smoke. It created a powerful new middle class, who inhabited new suburbs. It spawned working-class ghettoes that drew millions of people away from the countryside. It brought a new intensity to urban life and offered a vision of a relentlessly progressive future. It also made the transport of building materials from one town or city to another easy, bringing unfamiliar and disturbing architectural styles in its wake.

Stockton–Darlington railway
Opened in 1825, the Stockton and Darlington was the first public railway to use steam locomotives. These hauled coal trains between the two English towns. In 1830, the line was extended to the sea to bring coal to steam ships. In doing so, the railway created Middlesbrough, a new town.

Manchester mills
From the late 18th century, Manchester became the centre of manufactured cotton, its steam-powered mills pushing their way towards the old city centre. At its peak in the 1850s, when the Lancashire city hosted 108 mills, the textile trade declined from 1914. Surviving mills became factories, then flats and hotels.

Coal power
The image of primary-school-age children pushing and pulling wagons of coal in long, low and dangerous tunnels is a haunting reminder of how coal-powered manufacturing cities were rooted in the brutal exploitation of labour. As the 19th century progressed, cities of industry would become hotbeds of class strife.

Krupp Steel Works, Essen
Krupp Steel Works, founded in Essen in 1810 was the world's largest company within a biblical lifetime. It shaped an unholy urban landscape of tall smoking chimneys looming over enormous steel foundries and serried ranks of working-class barracks. During the Second World War, Krupp employed slave labour.

England

'And was Jerusalem builded here/Among these dark Satanic Mills?' To the poet William Blake, it seemed strange and sad that if Jesus Christ had come to Britain and walked its pastures green, rather than building a New Jerusalem in his honour, the country – 1,800 years later – had opted for a brutal, despiritualised way of ordering its economy, life and national soul. When Blake wrote these lines in 1804, British towns and cities were being truly revolutionised.

Victoria Street, Manchester
Arthur Fitzwilliam Tait's lithograph *Victoria Station, Manchester* (1848) depicts city merchants meeting in front of their new, commercial Italianate palazzi, while the medieval church tower is almost hidden from view and the clouded hills beyond are peppered with smoking chimneys.

Manchester Town Hall

Industry brought immense wealth to the English ruling class as well as to newly rich manufacturers and merchants. The scale of organisation necessary to run expanding industrial towns, as well as the wealth involved, is evoked by the Neo-Gothic extravagance of Manchester Town Hall (1877), designed by Alfred Waterhouse.

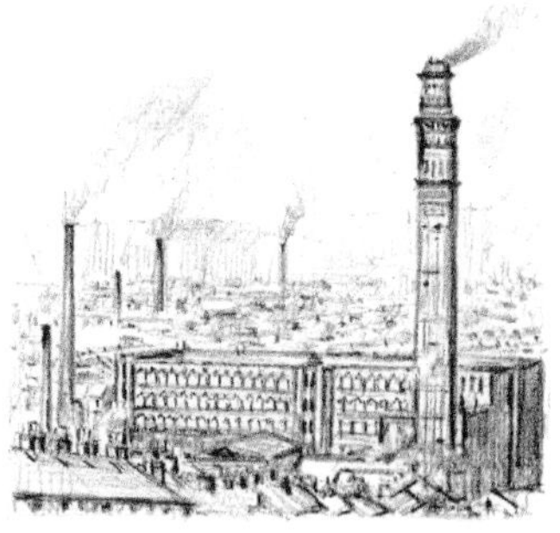

Wealth and poverty

Images of 19th-century Manchester reveal haunting contrasts between ambitious and opulent new public buildings, along with grand hotels and shopping parades, and the sulphurous squalor and degradation of the mills and working-class streets that made such civic munificence and consumer indulgence possible.

Birmingham

Birmingham was the fastest-growing 19th-century town. The delightful 18th-century market town, drawn by Thomas and Henry Archer in 1732, was to have changed out of all recognition within 60 years; by then Birmingham had been forged into the world's most important manufacturing centre.

Birmingham business boom

Birmingham became a city in 1889, yet by the late 20th century it was known to the wider world less for its cathedral – an upgraded Baroque parish church of 1725 – but for its Bull Ring and Rotunda, a brash 1960s commercial development celebrating car culture and the new consumerism.

Railway Towns

Swindon Railway Works
Swindon was a small Wiltshire market town before the coming of the Great Western Railway. Around its new locomotive works (1841–43) the GWR developed a paternalistic new town with handsome housing, church, pub, mechanics' institute, parks and a Victorian health service that was second to none.

Britain invented the steam railway locomotive and pioneered the world's first regular passenger steam railway – the Liverpool & Manchester in 1830 – and the first trunk, or long-distance express railway – the London & Birmingham in 1837. Railways did more than link towns and cities and boost trade between them; they shipped architectural ideas and building materials from one city to another, recasting the look of familiar streets in unfamiliar industrial bricks, stone and shiny marble.

The Great Western Railway (right)
The Great Western Railway was as much a religion as a commercial organisation. Here in 1860, its 4-2-2 express locomotive *Lord of the Isles* (exhibited at the Great Exhibition of 1851) stands outside the GWR's own church of St Mark's, Swindon (1845), designed by George Gilbert Scott and William Moffatt.

Grand Junction Railway, Crewe (left)
When the Grand Junction Railway opened its locomotive works at Monks Coppenhall near Crewe Hall, Cheshire, very few people lived in this remote rural area. Within a few years, and with the planning guidance of the GJR's chief engineer Joseph Locke, Crewe became a mighty centre of engineering and manufacturing.

Swindon Mechanics' Institute (right)
The Swindon Mechanics' Institute (1855) offered railway workers a self-improving reading room and lending library, lectures, healthcare, dances, concerts and theatrical productions. Closed in 1986 along with Swindon Works, it has been vandalised and set on fire several times. It may yet be saved.

Shipping

Clydeside, Glasgow
Clydeside is the name given to a long stretch of the River Clyde west of Glasgow that was once renowned for its inventive and prolific shipbuilding. The huge number of steamships launched here, from liners and freighters to Royal Navy warships, made Glasgow wealthy.

Shipyards were once a compelling feature of the world's great maritime cities. The Arsenale in Venice that built ships for the powerful Venetian Republic occupied more than a fifth of the city. And, yet, the industry became increasingly detached from the cities it made rich, so the sight of ships being constructed within sight of their centres became a rarity. As ports are pushed, wherever possible, ever further from cities, the connection between shipping and cities has become hidden.

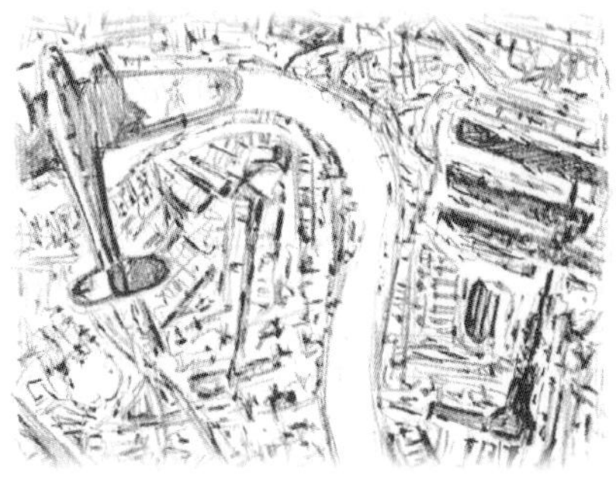

Helsinki South Harbour

Helsinki's South Harbour is located at the end of Eteläesplanadi, the city's premier shopping street, and alongside a popular market square. It remains a special place to watch the arrival and departure of the large passenger ships that ply the Baltic. Passengers can walk into the city's streets in minutes.

Isle of Dogs, London

London's docks were once very much a part of the city they served. The Isle of Dogs, seen here from the nosecone of a Heinkel 111 bomber as another below it prepares to unleash its weapons, was also densely populated: shipping was an intimate part of urban life.

Gdansk shipyards

The former Prussian and Lenin shipyards of Gdansk (Poland) are sited on an island within the city, a short walk from the magnificent medieval Gothic brick church of St Mary. It was here in 1980 that shipbuilders organised resistance against communist dictatorship.

Venice

Venice no longer builds ships other than gondolas and other small craft. The city, though, is now plagued by vast and determinedly ugly cruise liners – bling apartment-block hotels on water – that overpower its wondrous architecture and undermine their very foundations.

Soviet Industry

Magnitogorsk
Based loosely on Pittsburgh, Magnitogorsk is a giant steelwork city on the eastern edge of the Urals, built rapidly from the late 1920s. The German architect Ernst May attempted to create an ideal industrial city; it has become an object lesson in how not to design an industrial city.

When the Communists seized power in Russia in 1917, they moved quickly to establish the Soviet Union as an industrial power. A touch ironically, they worked with capitalist Americans to build giant factories, power stations and other industrial plants, while Vladimir Lenin, the Soviet leader who said 'Communism is Soviet power plus the electrification of the whole country' and who spoke of ending the separation of town from country, was driven from Moscow to his country estate in a Rolls-Royce.

Magnitogorsk (right)

The aim at Magnitogorsk had been to build a linear city with workers' housing following the line of the steelworks and separated from it by narrow green avenues. They would be able to walk to work. In the event, the need for fast roads meant that the city was more loosely planned.

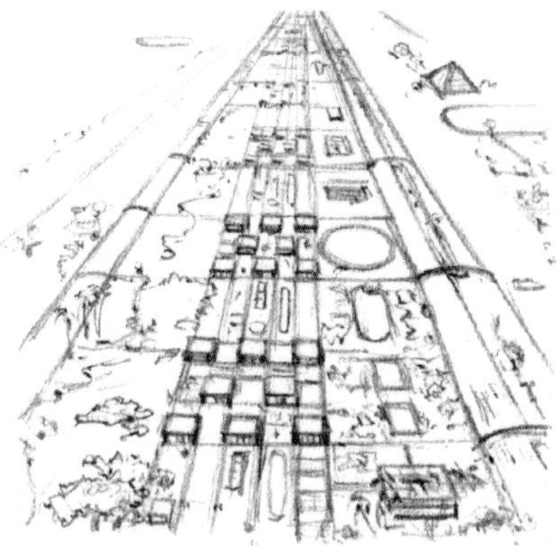

Soviet architecture (left)

Ideal workers' housing took the form of uniform ranks of low-quality concrete blocks. While these might have looked good, in an icy geometric fashion, on the architects' drawing boards, in reality they were isolated and rarely suited to the harsh climates of new Soviet cities.

Stalingrad (right)

Volgograd was once Stalingrad and before that Tsaritsyn. From 1925, Stalin set out to make the city a powerful industrial centre. Hitler had other ideas: Stalingrad was fought over savagely in 1942–43. After the Second World War it was rebuilt in the shadow of the giant victory sculpture, *The Motherland Calls*, and renamed Volgograd.

Steel Belt

Volkswagen factory, Wolfsburg
Steel also meant new weapons and, in Nazi Germany, regimented, mass-produced KdF Volkswagens (People's Cars), were made at a purpose-built factory in Wolfsburg (1938). A model village, Stadt des KdF Wagens, was built for the workforce.

It is hard to exaggerate just how revolutionary steel has been in the development of towns and cities worldwide. Attempts to produce pure steel from iron had been made through history – from *c.*1200 – and around the world, but in 1856 the English inventor Henry Bessemer succeeded in making mass-produced, low-cost steel a reality. Now faster, safer trains ran on steel rails, while the skyscraper soon followed along with so much of the complex infrastructure demanded by modern cities.

Mercedes-Benz, Stuttgart

The strength of German steel-based manufacturing was heavily advertised in city centres. A dominant Mercedes-Benz star crowns Stuttgart's castle-like Hauptbahnhof (Paul Bonatz, 1914–28). In Stuttgart, the car – despite environmental concerns – remains Kaiser, king and all princes.

BMW, Munich

BMW is to Munich what Mercedes-Benz is to Stuttgart. In 2007, the Bavarian car manufacturer opened BMW Welt. Designed by Viennese architects Coop Himmelb(l)au, this building offers three million visitors a year full-on immersion in the culture of BMW manufacturing and salesmanship.

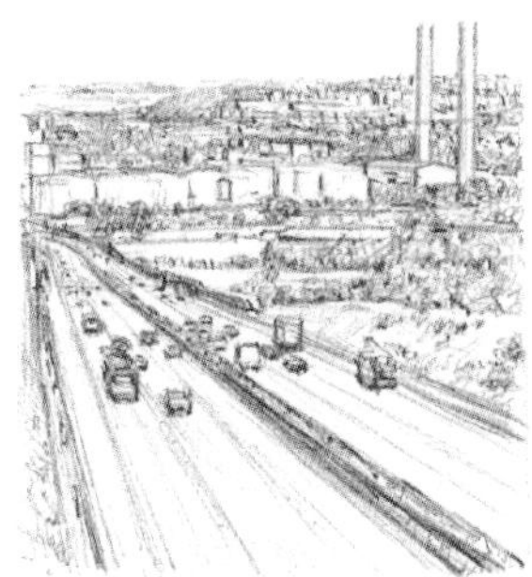

Autobahn network

The German autobahn network allows owners of BMW, Mercedes-Benz and other powerful cars to drive as fast as they choose, scything through the industrial steel belt and, as they do, demonstrating how manufacturing industry and the car were to re-make cities and urban life.

Autobahn development

The first stretch of German autobahn opened in 1935 between Darmstadt and Frankfurt am Main. Three years later, Rudolf Caracciola hurtled a streamlined Mercedes-Benz W125 along this stretch at 431 km/h (268 mph). Motorways allowed motorists to sweep past cities as if they were little more than names on exit signs.

USA

Detroit city centre
Detroit's New Center was built a little beyond the existing city centre in the 1920s. Its soaring architecture gave it the look and feel of a city in its own right. For 70 years, this early 'edge city' was effectively the campus of General Motors, the world's largest car manufacturer.

Industrialisation in the United States was executed on a titanic scale. Detroit, founded by the French adventurer Antoine de la Mothe Cadillac in 1701, became synonymous with car manufacturing when the company that bears Cadillac's name, along with the Ford Motor Company, set up shop here. Detroit became Motown. Along with Chicago, Cleveland, Cincinnati, Milwaukee and Cleveland, Detroit was the heartland of US manufacturing. As industry shifted elsewhere, this great stretch of North America became known as the Rust Belt.

Michigan Central Station

The astonishing high-rise Beaux Arts-style Michigan Central Station (1914) was once the gateway to the city of Detroit. In the mid-1950s when its centre was in full swing, Detroit had a fully employed population of 1.8 million. Sixty years later, this figure had fallen by 60 per cent. Central Station closed in 1988.

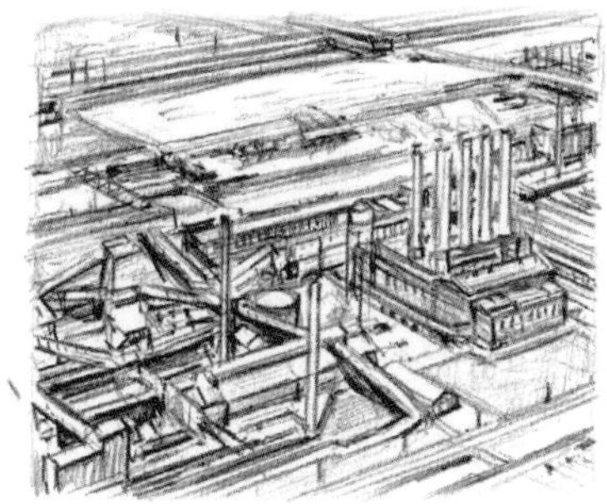

River Rouge Complex, Detroit

Ford's River Rouge Complex, ten miles west of Detroit at Dearborn on the Rouge River, was completed in 1928 to the designs of the prolific factory architect Albert Kahn who also built thousands of factories for Stalin's Russia. A *de facto* industrial city, Henry Ford employed 100,000 people here.

Schenectady, New York

Smaller and ultimately less vulnerable than Detroit, Schenectady, New York, became a manufacturing town with the opening of the Erie Canal in 1825 and the Mohawk and Hudson Railroad in 1831. The home of General Electric and the American Locomotive Company, it was 'the city that lights and hauls the world'.

Detroit in decline

Unprecedented industrial decline led the City of Detroit to declare bankruptcy in 2013. Manufacturing has shifted to China and South East Asia. In 2015, there were said to be 40,000 redundant buildings in Detroit, with many streets resembling scenes from disaster movies. Dependence on one industry is a dangerous thing.

Greening the Industrial City

Taiyuan
China's Shanxi province produces a quarter of the nation's coal. Its centre is Taiyuan, one of the world's most polluted industrial cities. Dense smogs smother the city – the last to stand against the Communists in the Civil War – for days on end. Coal remains emperor in Taiyuan.

'Forget six counties overhung with smoke/Forget the snorting steam and piston stroke/Forget the spreading of the hideous town …' wrote William Morris in his epic poem *The Earthly Paradise* (1870), by which time it was all but impossible to forget any of these Victorian intrusions. Industry pushed ahead with little regard for the health of towns and cities. The onward march of progress and profits were what mattered most. And, yet, Morris and fellow critics did engender concern for urban blight.

London fog

The 'pea-souper' smog that smothered central London in December 1952 killed 12,000 people in four days. Coal fires burned to keep London homes warm, adding to the worst smog on record. When this greasy miasma finally cleared, parliament set to work on the Clean Air Act of 1956.

Volkswagen, Dresden

Volkswagen's 'glass factory' in Dresden is a singularly clean, modern factory (Gunter Henn, 2002) devoted to the assembly of luxury cars, including Bentley Flying Spurs. Special freight-only trams deliver parts to the factory through the city centre. Set in parkland, this building is a very long way from Detroit.

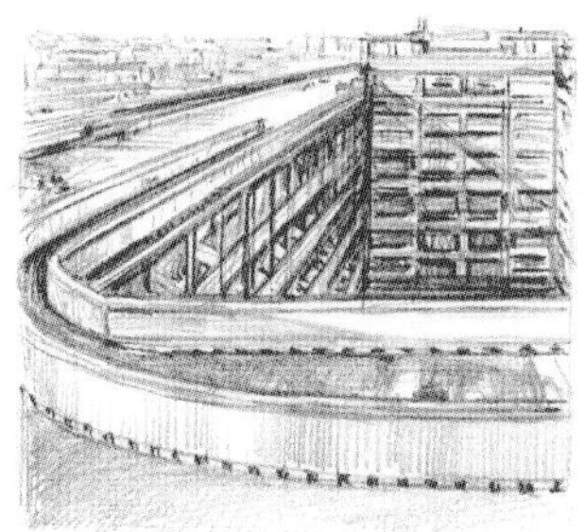

Lingotto car factory, Turin

Fiat's Lingotto car factory, Turin (Mattè Trucco, 1916–23) was a wonder of the industrial world. Cars were assembled over the levels up towards a test track circuiting its enormous roof. Closed in 1982, the factory has since been converted, by Renzo Piano, into a cultural centre for Turin and an automotive engineering school.

Mercedes-Benz Museum, Stuttgart

Close to the city centre, Stuttgart's enticing Mercedes-Benz Museum (UN Studio, 2006) stands by the entrance to the hallowed car factory. Its gleaming double-helix interior tells the story of 125 years of thoroughly well-engineered cars. Here, manufacturing and urban culture go piston-in-cylinder.

Introduction

Cities are centres of power whether for monarchs, dictators or elected governments. It is not difficult to make an educated guess as to which of these has commanded a particular city. Power does not always corrupt, yet when it is centralised you are almost certain to find lavish palaces facing vast squares laid out more for pomp, parades and soldiery than for commerce, entertainment and the common good. History, however, moves on, and the nature of such grandiloquent places softens.

Versailles
In 1682, Louis XIV, the Sun King, moved his court to Versailles. As his stupendous palace grew, so Versailles grew to a town of 60,000 people. The palace itself was a city of sorts, and anyone courting royal favour needed to make their way here rather than to Paris.

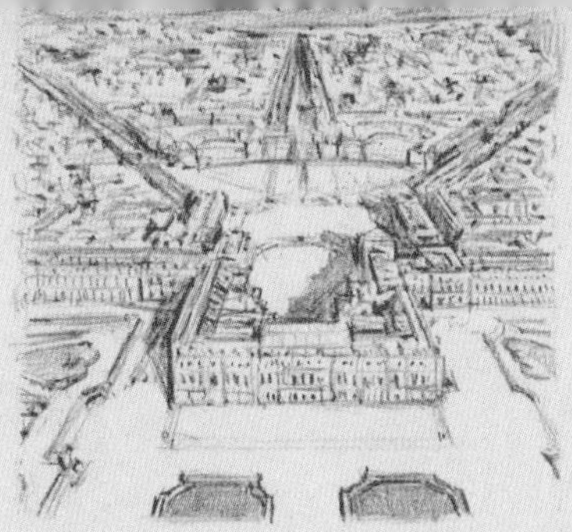

Court of the Sun King, Versailles
Although long discredited as a political system, the court of the Sun King retains its fascination. In 2008, a replica of a missing 15-ton gate, covered in 100,000 gold leaves at a cost of £4m and emblematic of Louis XIV's political persona, was installed in the heart of Versailles.

Palace of Versailles
The street pattern of Versailles is aligned with Louis XIV's palace. A trident of avenues spears towards the palace entrance and in every way the town is subservient to its royal master. The grounds of the palace cover an area greater than the landmass of Manhattan.

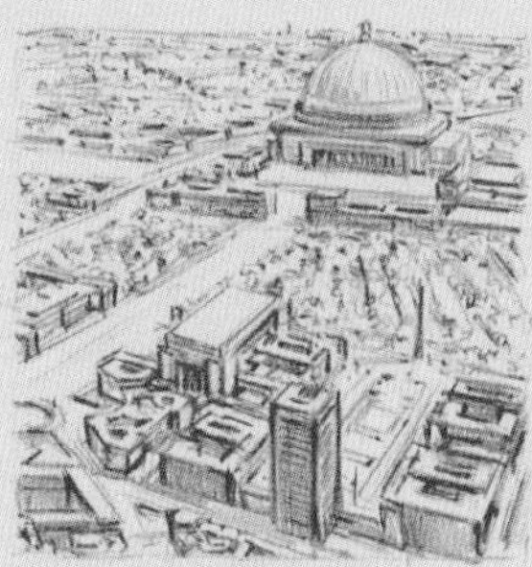

Metropolitan Cathedral, Paris
Seven years before the French Revolution, the Neo-Classical architect Étienne-Louis Boullée drew this perspective of an incomprehensibly massive Metropolitan Cathedral for Paris. It was a fantasy and not some royal commission from Louis XVI, but it was to inspire Adolf Hitler's court architect, Albert Speer.

'World Capital Germania'
'As world capital Berlin will only be comparable with ancient Egypt, Babylon and Rome! What is London, what is Paris compared to that!' Between 1937 and 1943, Albert Speer built a giant model of a proposed replacement for Berlin: this was Hitler's Brobdingnagian 'World Capital Germania'.

British Empire

New Delhi
Although the most impressive marriage of Indian and British architectural styles is to be found in the design of the Viceroy's House (1912–29), New Delhi, its architect Edwin Lutyens had originally intended no such thing. Referring to 'Moghul tosh', he said 'they want me to do Hindu – *Hindon't*, I say'.

Unlike the Romans, or the French many centuries later, the British made little or no attempt to establish an imperial style of architecture and culture in its widespread colonial towns and cities. While it was unsurprising to find 18th-century colonial governors' buildings – seats of local power – as replicas of familiar English country houses, these gave way to variations on local themes and, eventually, to fascinating fusions of very different design traditions – those of Britain, its colonies, dominions and protectorates.

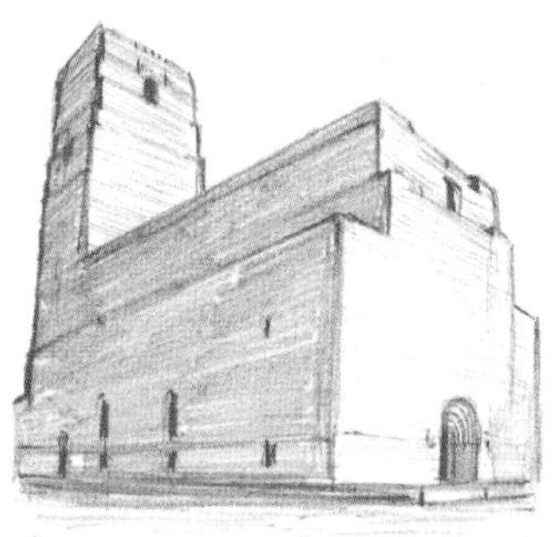

St Martin's Garrison Church, New Delhi

St Martin's Garrison Church (1930), New Delhi, was designed by Lutyens's assistant Arthur Shoosmith. A marvel of brick and concrete construction, it is at once raw, elemental, and powerful and – inside – cool in the Delhi heat under Wren-like saucer domes. A military, ecclesiastical and civic masterpiece.

Old Delhi

Congested and seemingly chaotic from an urban planning point of view, Old Delhi was the capital of Moghul India. Founded by Shah Jahan in 1639, it boasted munificent forts, palaces, markets, tombs and grand civic spaces. But, as few people were prepared to live outside its walls, it became overcrowded.

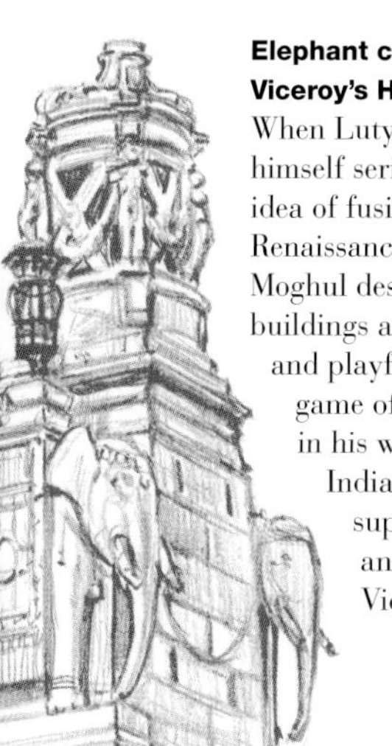

Elephant column, Viceroy's House, New Delhi

When Lutyens applied himself seriously to the idea of fusing European Renaissance and Hindu and Moghul design, he produced buildings at once magnificent and playful – 'the high game of architecture' in his words. Sculpted Indian elephants support corners and columns of the Viceroy's House.

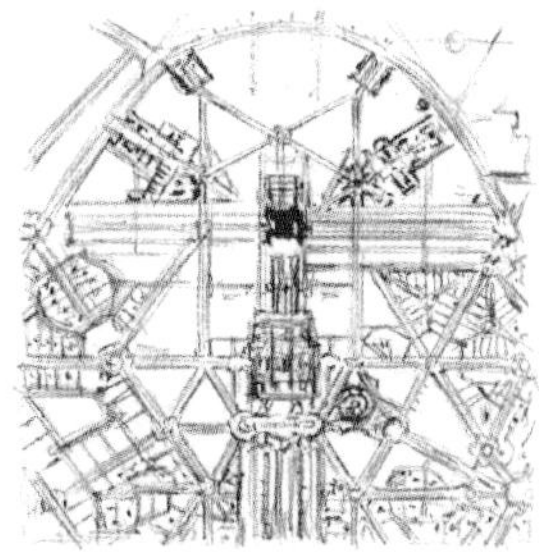

New Delhi plan

In 1911, King George V laid the foundation stone of a new Indian capital, New Delhi. Planned in grand Beaux Arts style, with radiating avenues and far-reaching vistas, by Edwin Lutyens, this magnificent design has lent itself to great architecture, parades, ceremonies and, since 1947, a sense of Indian nationhood.

Brasilia

Main axis

The principal street of Brasilia is a long axis leading from the commercial zone of the city, through its diplomatic and cultural quarters, to its political hub focused on the twin towers of the Congress building. Brasilia is the country's fastest-growing city with the highest GDP in Latin America.

In 1956, Juscelino Kubitschek, the dynamic new president of Brazil promised 'fifty years of progress in five'. Key to this rapid acceleration was the creation of Brasilia. Rio de Janeiro had been the Brazilian capital from 1763, yet the first republican constitution of 1891 promised a new capital in the centre of the country. Lúcio Costa planned Brasilia, Roberto Burle Marx landscaped it and Oscar Niemeyer designed its monumental buildings: Brasilia was inaugurated within four years.

The National Congress Building (right))

The National Congress Building (Oscar Niemeyer, 1957–64) was designed so that those who voted senators and deputies into office could walk on the roofs above the debating chambers and executive offices. They were the masters, the politicians their elected servants, a situation destined not to last.

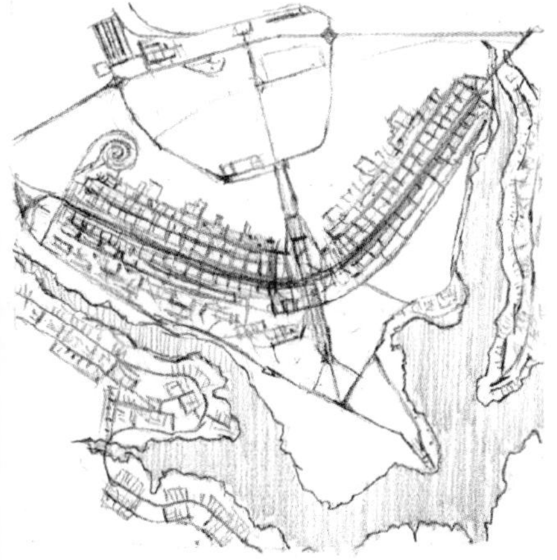

Brasilia town layout (left)

Seen from the air, the plan of Brasilia resembles either a giant aircraft or huge bird coming to land by Lago Paranoá, an artificial lake surrounded by country clubs, restaurants, embassies and a marina. Significantly, many politicians, diplomats and civil servants abandon Brasilia, by plane, for Rio on weekends.

The Alvorada Palace (right)

'What is Brasilia,' asked President Kubitschek, 'if not the dawn of a new day for Brazil?' Ever since, the exquisite Palácio da Alvorada (Palace of the Dawn; Oscar Niemeyer, 1958), sited on a peninsula jutting into Lake Paranoá, has been the official home of Brazil's head of state.

Authoritarian Capitals

Ceausescu's palace, Bucharest
Nicolae Ceausescu, president of Romania, mass murderer and Knight Grand Cross of the Most Honourable Order of the Bath, had the People's Palace (Anca Petrescu, 1984–97) built over historic residential areas of Bucharest. Seventy per cent of this Communist carbuncle remains empty today.

Dictators and authoritarian regimes tend to shape cities in a monumental manner. Principal streets, public squares and presidential palaces are realised on a scale aimed at outdoing the wildest dreams of Roman emperors. The idea is to demonstrate the might of a particular regime, to cow citizens and to suggest – in tiers of brick, stone, concrete and marble – that here are buildings and places that will last a thousand years, along with the infallible regimes that ordered them. As these regimes are brittle, so they tend to crack and fall along with their monuments.

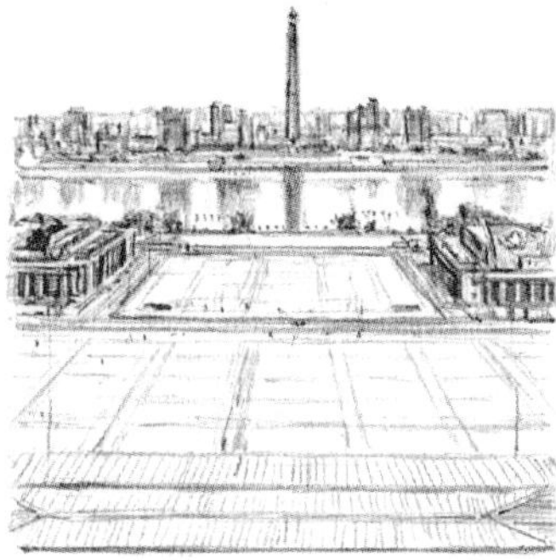

Kim Il-sung Square, Pyongyang
Choreographed rallies of 100,000 people frequently fill Pyongyang's Kim Il-sung Square, a public space opened in 1954, modelled on Tiananmen Square, Beijing. It faces the Juche Tower (1982), a monument representing North Korean ideology, across the Taedong River.

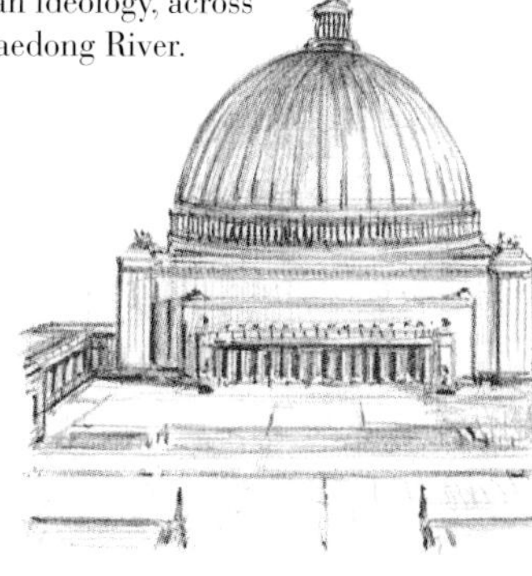

Volkshalle, Berlin
Albert Speer's proposed Volkshalle boasted the world's biggest dome. If it had been built, and when it was filled with 180,000 sieg-heiling Nazis, clouds would have formed inside. The Thousand Year Reich that this Boullée-like building was to have celebrated, however, missed its target by 988 years.

Red Square, Moscow
Ivan the Terrible cleared the area known since the 1660s as Red Square (from *krasnaya* meaning 'red', in other words, beautiful) to give the Kremlin's guns a clear line of shot. A sacred and secular space, from the Communist era it was also a place to display dead leaders and military hardware.

Palace of the Soviets, Moscow
'Don't be scared of height!' said Stalin. The 1932 design by Boris Iofan et al for a Palace of the Soviets, Moscow, was revised to outdo the Empire State Building. A 100-m (328-ft) statue of Lenin replaced that of a 'free proletarian' on top. War stopped Stalin's architectural game in 1941.

Introduction

Even before the first towns and cities existed, humans dreamed of what the perfect settlement might be like. You need only to look at indigenous settlements discovered in the depths of the Brazilian rainforest by the outside world in recent years to understand how important pattern and order are to people. The plans of such villages are natural yet thoroughly thought through, some resembling the female uterus with its promise of warmth and security as well as fecundity, birth and new life.

The Ideal City
Plato's Republic was concerned with notions of the ideal city. As classical scholarship blossomed in Renaissance Italy in the 15th century, the theme became popular among artists and architects. They included Luciano Laurana, who may have painted this ideal city when working on the Palazzo Ducale, Urbino.

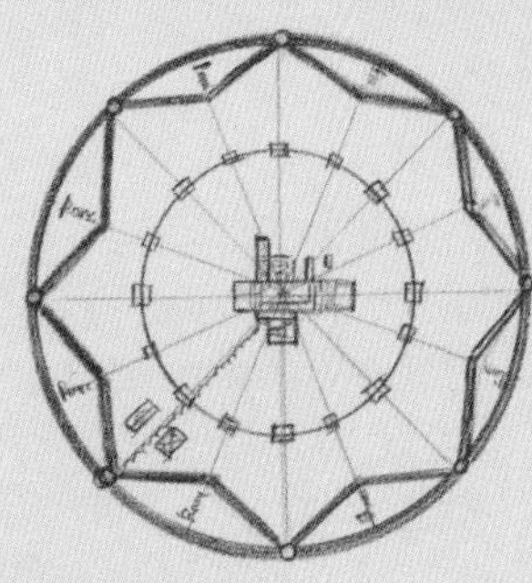

Sforzinda

Sforzinda is an imaginary 15th-century ideal Italian town or city designed by Antonio di Pietro Averlino in the pattern of an eight-pointed star set within a circle. Streets radiate out from three central squares – palace, cathedral and market – and every second street runs on either side of a canal.

Palmanova

Palmanova is Sforzinda realised. Vincenzo Scamozzi designed this nine-pointed ideal Venetian fortress town with the military architect Giulio Savorgnan. Built between 1593 and 1813, at first no Venetians wanted to live here. In 1622, criminals were offered a pardon if they were prepared to settle in Palmanova.

Urbino

Federico da Montefeltro was the Duke of Urbino who devoted his magnanimous mid-15th-century rule to making Urbino an ideal Renaissance city. However, Urbino was not planned on a strict geometrical and cosmological basis like Sforzinda and Palmanova: it was more organic, more humanistic and, ultimately, more liveable.

The City of To-Morrow

The City of To-Morrow and Its Planning was a 1929 English translation of the radical Swiss-French architect Le Corbusier's visions of the ideal 20th-century city. Compared at the time to Freud, Picasso and Einstein, Le Corbusier differed from his fellow geniuses by his insistence on strict, ideal urban order.

Pre-industrial

Main Square, Pienza
Pope Pius XII, born in Corsignano, Tuscany, in 1405, rebuilt the town, with the architect Bernardo Rossellino, along the lines of an ideal Renaissance town. Renamed Pienza, it boasts a grand centre and heroic architecture very different in scale and ambition from most Tuscan hill towns.

Ideal towns based on Italian Renaissance theories were built in their entirety sometimes, as Palmanova demonstrates. For the most part, though, such ideals were put into practice in piecemeal or less dogmatic fashion. Because towns and cities evolve in an organic rather than a mechanistic manner, plans based purely on pure ideals are unlikely to work – for robots, yes, but for human beings, no. Between 1500 and 1800, however, such ideals informed the work of distinguished urban planners and enlightened clients.

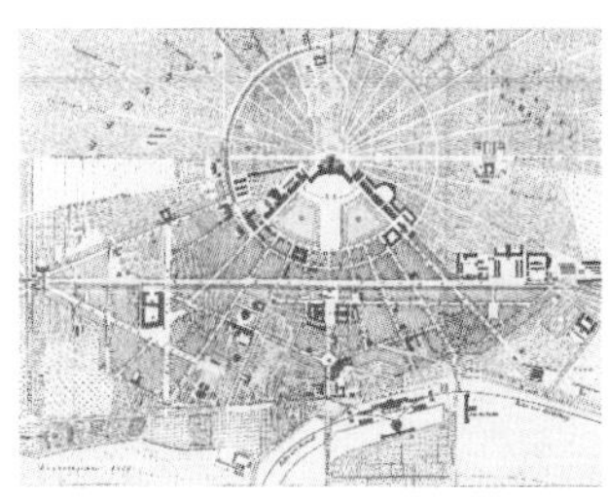

Karlsruhe
Karl Wilhelm von Baden founded the new capital of the newly created Grand Duchy of Baden in 1715. The German town fanned out along 32 streets radiating from Wilhelm's Palace. Formalised, with Neo-Classical buildings by the architect Friedrich Weinbrenner in 1797, the striking plan and classical character of Karlsruhe endure.

Aquae Sulis, Bath
The former Roman spa Aquae Sulis became England's most fashionable town outside London in the 18th century, when it was developed into a showcase of classical planning and architecture by John Wood the Elder. Bath's honey-coloured stone terraces, circus and crescents danced decorously around a beautiful natural setting.

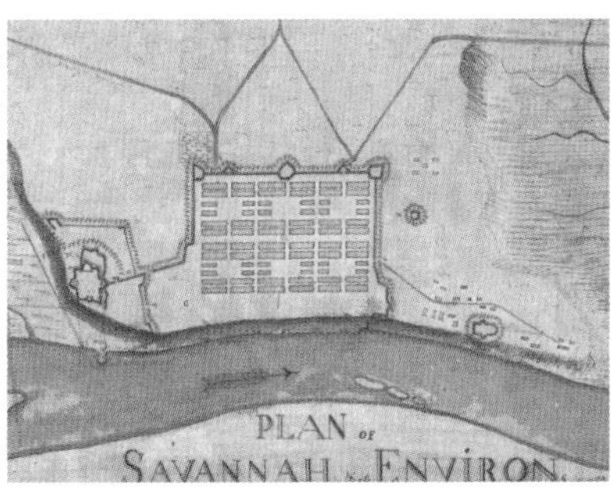

Savannah, Georgia
A grid of axial streets and garden squares, Savannah, Georgia, was laid out in 1733 to designs by the settlement's founder, James Oglethorpe, an English soldier, parliamentarian and philanthropist. Each square acts as a microcosm of the city as a whole, so that Savannah could be extended in uniform fashion.

Edinburgh New Town
Edinburgh New Town, a magnificent classical foil to the medieval Old Town's broadsword, has been called 'the Scottish Enlightenment in Stone'. In 1766 James Craig, a 26-year-old architect, won the competition for its axial design. Graceful and beautifully executed, it remains a powerful expression of 18th-century ideals.

Romantic

Ramsgate
In the 1840s, Augustus Welby Pugin (1812–52), a fiery young English architect, polemicist and zealous Catholic convert, built his house and church at Ramsgate on the Kent coast. A Benedictine monastery, by Pugin's sons, followed: here, in miniature, was the kernel of a revived medieval English ecclesiastical town.

As 19th-century industry swept through the developing world, almost inevitably there was a reaction to the dirt, poverty and ugliness this furiously fast-paced revolution brought in its prodigious wake. While some Romantic-era writers, theorists and architects harked back to the golden age of 'Merrie England' and its equivalent in other heavily industrialised countries, philanthropic industrialists constructed ideal new manufacturing villages. There were also lessons from picture-book colonial settlements where gentler industries, like viniculture, had taken root.

Portmeirion

Portmeirion is an impish Welsh holiday village set above Dwyryd estuary. Built between 1925 and 1975 by the Welsh architect Clough Williams-Elli in the guise of a colourful Italian hill town, it is a charming, yet educational, riposte to the nominally rational architecture and soulless planning of modern towns.

Port Sunlight

Every house in Port Sunlight, an industrial garden village on the Wirral Peninsula, Cheshire, is different. William Lever, soap magnate and philanthropist, employed more than 30 architects between 1888 and 1914 to shape well-crafted homes for 3,500 employees, along with a swimming pool, concert hall, art gallery, church and schools.

Stellenbosch

Founded in 1679, Stellenbosch was a Dutch colonial farming village on South Africa's Western Cape that grew rapidly into a successful wine-growing town. Its agricultural legacy shows in the beautiful, yet simple, gabled white farmhouses set back from streets and enjoying ample green space: an African garden town.

New Lanark

From 1800, New Lanark, a mill town established along the River Clyde in 1786, became a profitable experiment in utopian socialism when Robert Owen, industrialist and social reformer, took control. Clean factories, decent housing and Britain's first infants' school were notable achievements. New Lanark is a tourist attraction today.

Twentieth-century Dreams

Disneyland, Anaheim
Walt Disney's Disneyland at Anaheim opened in 1955, ten years after the end of the Second World War. Architecturally, this theme park, or make-believe town, was crowned by Sleeping Beauty's Castle, a play on the 15th-century French Château d'Ussé and the 19th-century Bavarian fantasia, Neuschwanstein.

Dominated by two world wars that devastated and destroyed entire towns and the cities, the 20th century was a time for both reflection and re-invention. While ever more time and urban space was devoted to industry and the car, and as ever more cities became entangled with new roads and choked by new forms of pollution, new solutions were sought and invented: new forms of industrial towns, new ways of housing the industrial working class and fresh escapist fantasias. Step by step, many historic city centres are beginning to resemble theme parks.

Napier (right)

Founded on Hawke's Bay, New Zealand, in the 1850s, Napier was destroyed by an earthquake in 1931. The town was rebuilt in Art Deco style and, despite dim-witted demolitions between the 1960s and 1990s, the seaside town is a World Heritage Site today, its tourism based on its sunshine architecture.

Fordlandia (left)

Fordlandia was built in Brazil's Amazonian rainforest from 1928 to supply the Ford Motor Company with rubber. A replica of a Detroit suburb it offered free housing, food and healthcare, but permitted no alcohol, sex or fun. The indigenous workforce found it uninhabitable. A total disaster, it was abandoned in 1945.

Les Espaces d'Abraxas (right)

The centre of the Parisian new town Marne-la-Vallée is dominated by Les Espaces d'Abraxas – monumental, postmodern classical, pre-fabricated concrete housing blocks of the early 1980s, designed by Ricardo Bofill's Taller de Arquitectura. Here is ancient Rome revisited on behalf of 20th-century French working class.

Introduction

Metropolis
Fritz Lang's epochal film *Metropolis* (1927) set the tone for the look and feel of imaginary dystopian cities of the future. These were ideal cities seen through a glass darkly, reflecting a growing concern that industrialism and automation were ultimately inhumane.

Ideal cities were as much a literary as a strictly architectural concern. From the Renaissance, new, revolutionary and even madcap ideas for reinventing the city were formed in polemics and novels. Artists, too, contributed ideas to encourage architects and patrons to think differently. And, yet, because cities are largely organisms that develop as trade, industry and populations rise and fall, and because of their sheer scale, ideals rarely work as planned, proving fascinating yet too constraining for urban growth and change.

Utopia

Thomas More's *Utopia* of 1516 is a curious book. Part polemic, part satire, it imagines an island with 54 uniform cities ordered along ideal lines and without private property. Everyone works, meals are communally served, there is no need for locks on doors and citizens abide by rules.

Laputa (below)

Laputa is a flying island city populated by astronomers, mathematicians, musicians and technologists so lost in thought and ideals that they are unable to build in straight lines: Laputa is not known for its architecture. It is, of course, a satirical invention of Jonathan Swift in *Gulliver's Travels* (1726).

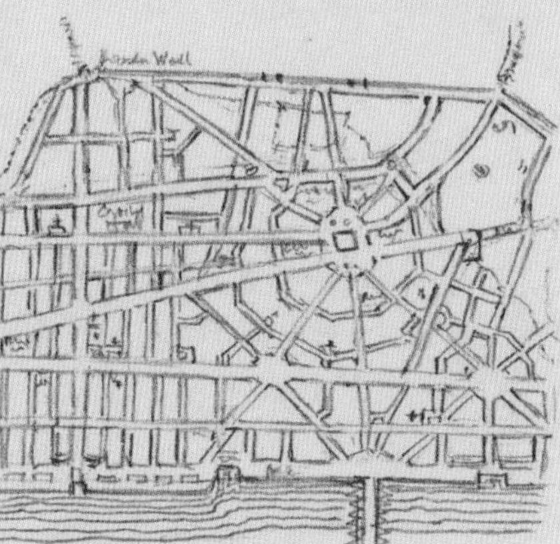

London re-modelled? (above)

After the Great Fire of London of 1666, Christopher Wren drew up a rational, Renaissance plan for the city. Centred on a grand avenue between St Paul's Cathedral and the Royal Exchange it was shelved because the City of London was in a hurry to get back to work.

New World Ideals

National Mall, Washington DC
An enormously dignified processional way through the US capital, the National Mall, Washington DC, is a monumental avenue stretching 3 km (2 miles) from the Capitol to the Lincoln Memorial. First planned in 1791, the Mall was reconsidered and extended in the early 1850s and again in 1901.

America, the new-found land, promised religious and intellectual freedom, personal liberty and a remarkable opportunity for disaffected, disinherited and jobless Europeans to start all over again in a new country. It was also an opportunity to design new towns that would later become cities on idealistic lines. While some new settlements developed organically with no overarching plan, others demonstrated blueprints for social order reflecting a desire by their citizens to establish codified patterns for living and future development in a largely unknown world.

Lincoln Memorial, Washington DC
The Lincoln Memorial, Washington DC (Henry Bacon, 1922), is where in 1963 Martin Luther King gave his 'I Have a Dream' speech. Some wanted a log cabin to represent Abraham Lincoln but this Doric temple symbolises an American belief in democracy rooted in ancient Athens.

New Haven, Connecticut
English Puritans founded New Haven, Connecticut and its theocratic government in 1638. John Brockett laid out a grid of streets centred on a green public square that is still very much in evidence today. This ideal town, now a city, has been home to Yale University since 1701.

Las Vegas
Incorporated as a city in 1911 and wreathed in neon lights since the 1930s, Las Vegas, Nevada, calls itself 'the entertainment capital of the world'. It is also known as 'Sin City', and is famous for its extravagant architecture, an oasis of sorts in the expanse of the Mojave Desert.

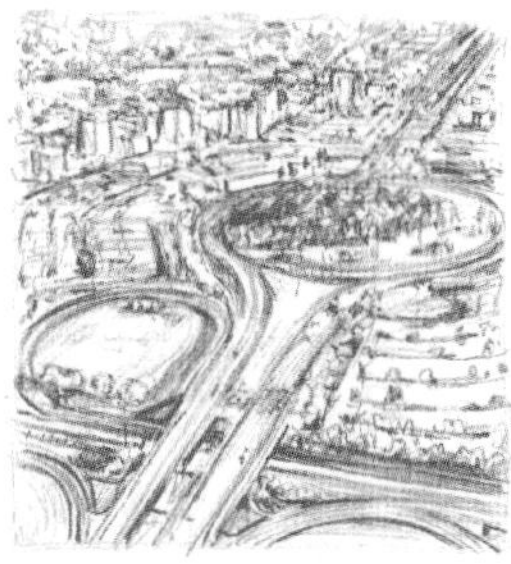

Canberra
Indifferent new buildings have done their best to undermine the skyline of Canberra in recent decades. On the ground, however, Walter Burley Griffin and Marion Mahony Griffin's 1911 competition-winning plan for the new Australian capital, with its wealth of trees and constellation-like street pattern, is still evident.

Ideal Regional Cities

During the colonial era it was easy for European administrations to impose new towns and cities on countries that, climatically and culturally, were very different from those found, for example, in Britain or France. Equally, newly independent countries were often in danger of importing unsuitable plans and designs for new towns and cities, either because these appeared enticingly modern or because they lacked local professional skills. Sometimes, though both imperial and independent governments created ideal towns with imagination and empathy.

Chandigarh
'Let this be . . . symbolic of the freedom of India unfettered by the traditions of the past,' proclaimed Jawaharlal Nehru, independent India's first prime minister, when he announced Chandigarh the new capital of East Punjab. Le Corbusier's sculpture of an open hand symbolises the city's willingness to give and to receive.

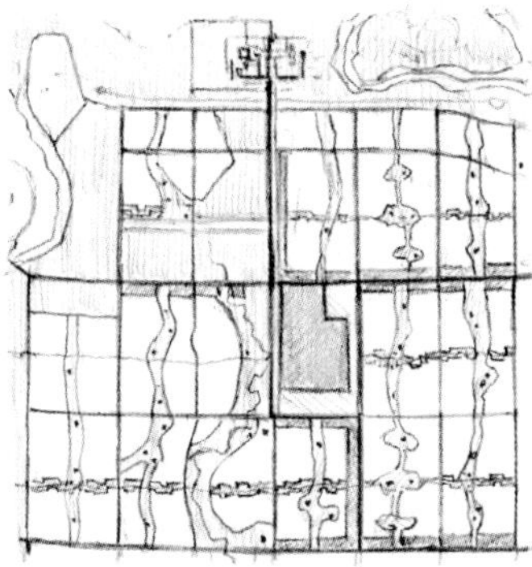

Chandigarh plan

The original plan for Chandigarh, drawn up from 1947 by the Polish architect Maciej Nowicki and US planner Albert Mayer was fan-shaped. Le Corbusier revised this after Nowicki's death in 1950, employing a gridiron plan that, in practice, proved subtle and adaptable and was laced with sun, space and greenery.

Palace of the Assembly, Chandigarh

Le Corbusier's Palace of the Assembly (1953–63) is one of several striking sculptural monuments the Swiss-French architect designed for the low-rise garden city. Although India's most prosperous city today, Chandigarh is being stripped of its heritage as Le Corbusier-designed furniture, fittings, prints and drawings are sold abroad.

Asmara heritage

Asmara remains a tolerant city where the bells of Roman Catholic and Coptic churches mingle with calls to prayers by muezzins. Its complex heritage is reflected in the name of its principal, palm-lined street: what had been Mussolini, Queen Victoria and Haile Selassie Avenue is now Independence Avenue.

Asmara development

Between 1935 and 1941, the Italian government invested money and talent in the development of Asmara, capital of Eritrea, and especially so in modern architecture. The result is a highland city (elevation 2,325 m/7,628 ft) of remarkable grace, sophistication, greenery, uncompromised pre-war Modernity and 1930s Italian coffee bars.

Modern Movement Ideals

Cité Le Corbusier
Le Corbusier's hugely controversial high-rise Plan Voison of 1925, envisaging the demolition of much of Paris north of the Seine, was never built. What he did build was the Cité de Refuge (1933), a hostel for the Salvation Army that, however flawed, was a model for much modern urban housing.

Immediately after the First World War there was a desire among many architects, planners, artists, intellectuals and even city governments to lay the foundations for a new world, washing away the vestiges of the *ancien regimes* that had brought such terrible death and destruction, along with mud and carnage, to the world. Here, perhaps, was the opportunity to begin afresh, to build bright, white, clean and rational cities speaking of modern order, enlightenment and civilisation from the ashes of 1914–18. And, yet, it was only after the Second World War that Modern Movement ideals truly revolutionised urban design.

Tel Aviv modernity (right)
The Nazis abhorred modernism in almost any form except factories and weapons. Jewish architects who escaped Hitler's Germany in the 1930s and settled in Palestine transformed the beginnings of Tel Aviv, a new garden city planned by Patrick Geddes, a Scot, into a remarkable expression of Bauhaus design.

Zlin (left)
Zlin, a Moravian town, was transformed by Tomas Bata, the shoemaker who set up shop here in 1894. Bata created a new garden city for his workforce with factories and houses alike designed according to the same factory aesthetic. The plan was by Frantisek Gahura, a student of Le Corbusier.

Stuttgart's Bauhaus influences (right)
In 1927, the city of Stuttgart funded an exhibition of ideal new homes curated by Ludwig Mies van der Rohe for the Deutscher Werkbund. Designed by the best rising modernists from across Europe, the radical, Bauhaus-influenced houses were visited by half a million people.

Introduction

Mexico City
Rising from the ruins of Aztec Tenochtitlan, Mexico City sprawls to an improbable degree today. The population of Greater Mexico is more than 21 million and growing fast; its economy is equal to that of entire Latin American countries. Third-rate development and shanty towns stretch as far as the imagination dares allow.

The majority of the world's most populous cities, even if they have grown from planned centres, have tended to sprawl and notably so since the 1950s. This is partly because economic centralisation has drawn ever-increasing numbers of people to cities, and partly because the car has encouraged streets and homes to stretch ever further from old urban centres. Even so, there are cities that seem to revel in sprawl and that appear to have little taste for rational planning. Sprawl is a disease of sorts, causing cities to become functionally and environmentally unsustainable, or else splintering into smaller centres.

São Paulo

The density of São Paulo, Brazil – twice that of Paris – is such that the city has 10,000 miles of streets, bursting at the seams with skyscrapers. Such is the draw of the largest city in the southern hemisphere that today it is flanked by desperately poor shanty towns.

Atlanta

A major transportation hub since 1837, Atlanta, Georgia has been a long-standing economic success, yet, since 1987 suburban sprawl has seen the region lose 20 hectares (50 acres) of tree cover a day. Home to the world's busiest airport, Atlanta continues to expand despite concerns over water supplies and pollution.

Urban sprawl, Houston

Sprawl may not be pretty, but, as people say in Houston, Texas, it appears to work. In 2014 alone this oil city issued 64,000 permits for new homes along its infinite freeways. The city's economy continues to grow now that it is diversifying; it will sprawl much further yet.

Santiago de Chile sewage treatment

In 2012 Santiago de Chile became the first major Latin American city to treat 100 per cent of its sewage, a key moment for a city squeezed between mountains and ocean. The city has sprawled considerably, yet in recent decades has also done much to improve public transport and reduce pollution.

Steady Growth

London suburbs
London's suburbs grew in concentric rings around the city. A real effort was made from the late 19th century to plan these, so that many were either *de facto* or *de jure* garden suburbs rather than unmitigated sprawl. Not, of course, all of them. Sprawl, too often, rules here.

Perhaps the most successful organic, or partly planned, cities are those that have grown more or less steadily. However, even London, often held up as an exemplar of gradual growth experienced extremely rapid population growth between 1800 and 1914. What, London, among certain other major cities, enjoys, however, is greenery – gardens, parks and a sense that, if not contained, modern sprawl is pruned, tamed and that little bit more civilised than it is in other cities that have simply let rip.

Vancouver

Vancouver, founded in 1886, is Canada's most densely occupied municipality. It is often named as one of the best cities in which to live. This, perhaps, is because no matter how many people settle here, it is contained happily by mountains, parks, forests and the Pacific Ocean.

Tokyo sprawl

Tokyo grew rapidly in the 20th century. Houses on individual plots occupied huge swathes of territory, and yet unlike US cities, for example, most development took place along suburban railway lines rather than freeways. Sprawl here is intimately linked to commuting.

Berlin

Berlin is essentially a low-rise city, interspersed by parks, gardens, lakes and rivers. During the years of Communist rule after the fall of the Third Reich, attempts were made to transform East Berlin into a city of largely indifferent towers and densely occupied housing blocks. That experiment is over.

Toronto development

Set in former Iroquois territory, Toronto is Canada's most populous city. Its suburbs have often been planned, so that the city has expanded even in recent years in a largely generous and well-mannered fashion. Nature intrudes in the city's downtown grid in the guise of deep ravines.

Developing World

Lagos
Once largely confined to a Nigerian lake island, Lagos has sprawled into the hinterland on a massive scale. This, one of Africa's fastest-growing cities, has a population of approximately 20 million. An over-reliance on oil, roads and cars has led to widespread congestion and pollution.

If sprawl is barely contained in the world's most advanced cities, and largely unchecked in much of North and South America, in poorer and less certain parts of the world, it is a shocking phenomenon. Unrestrained population growth, the lure of potential work and the abandonment of traditional village life and agriculture have led to a situation where today, for the first time in history, more than half the world's population lives in cities, a proportion set to rise ever higher in the future.

Dhaka
When Dhaka became the capital of a newly independent Bangladesh in 1971, its population was 1.3 million. Forty years later, it had grown to 15 million. Although far more densely occupied than even Hong Kong, sheer numbers have seen this poor city sprawl north to south along the Buriganga River.

Johannesburg
Johannesburg boomed rapidly with the development of gold mines from the mid-1880s. Still booming in many ways, its success has attracted a large population of rural poor: 30 per cent of Jo'bergers live in 'informal dwellings' Suburbs range from the plush and gated to the most basic shanty towns.

Istanbul influx
Just a quarter of Istanbul's population (14.5 million) was born in the great Turkish city straddling the Bosphorus. Huge immigration, mainly from eastern Turkey, has changed the face of this once magnificent city and seen it stretch interminably in poorly arraigned ranks of the dreariest buildings.

Cairo
Known as Umm al-Dunya ('Mother of the World'), Cairo is a fecund city that has sprawled in barely contained fashion despite the construction of planned satellite towns. Famed for its ancient heart, nevertheless one building in five here is less than 15 years old.

Introduction

Cité Soleil

Set at one end of Haiti's international airport, Cité Soleil is the archetypal shanty town. Some 400,000 people live here in extreme poverty. There is no sewage system. Two-thirds of the makeshift homes are without a latrine. Crime is endemic. Vicious armed gangs rule except when UN troops do the rounds.

Townships. Barrios. Favelas. Young Towns. Tent Cities. Trailer Parks. Villas Miserias. These are all terms for shanty towns, a name probably derived from the French Canadian *chantier*, a winter station for lumberjacks. Shanty towns, however, are mostly associated with countries much hotter and very much poorer than Canada. They tend to emerge from a ragtag tangle of makeshift building materials wherever there is a rush to cities unable to cope with the demand for instant new housing, civic services and infrastructure.

La Rocinha, Rio de Janeiro
La Rocinha is Brazil's largest favela. Winding up a steep hillside overlooking the beaches of Rio de Janeiro its population numbers anywhere between 70,000 and 180,000. In recent years, electricity, running water, shops, schools and public services have transformed it into a ramshackle urban village.

Ciudad Bolivar, Bogota
Despite attempts to urbanise the Bogota barrio Ciudad Bolivar, this remains a poor and dangerous hillside settlement of 700,000 people. Inordinately high birth rates – one in five adolescent girls is a mother – spells a very young population (70 per cent under 30) and rising demand for public services.

Villa Carton, Buenos Aires
When, in 2007, fire swept through Villa Carton, a Buenos Aires villa miseria housed under a flyover, residents were promised a brave new home. This proved to be a slightly updated version of Villa Carton, lacking what charm it had. Today, 120,000 people in the Argentinian capital live in shanty towns.

Makoko floating school, Lagos
That architectural ingenuity can raise the quality of life in shanty towns is demonstrated, practically and delightfully, by the floating school (2012) designed by NLE Architects to cope with high winds and floods for Makoko, a waterside settlement with a population of 100,000 on stilts on the edge of Lagos.

Developed World

Cañada Real, Madrid
Within walking distance of some of Europe's finest and most prosperous streets and squares, Cañada Real Galiana is a 40-year-old shanty town disgracing Madrid. Home to 40,000 people who rebuild their homes when the authorities demolish them, this is the centre of the city's drug trade.

Shanty towns are not confined to poor and developing countries. In Europe, they exist for a number of reasons, ranging from that of desperate people trying to escape poverty, savage politics and religious extremism in other parts of the world to those of lifestyle choices made by alternative, drop-out communities. Mostly, though, shanty towns exist wherever large numbers of people make beelines to economically successful cities that are nevertheless unable to cope with the flow of human traffic.

Sangatte

Sangatte is the French village near Calais where Louis Bleriot made the first crossing of the English Channel by powered aircraft in 1909. Today it is better known for its notorious refugee camp, closed in 2002, for asylum seekers hoping to get to Britain. A new camp opened in 2015.

Patras

One of the first European ports of call for refugees escaping Africa, Asia and the Middle East is the Greek port of Patras. In 2009, Greek police demolished a 'city' that included a mosque, built largely by Afghans from flotsam combed from beaches.

Deponija, Belgrade

Refugees, many of them Roma, from the fallout of the Kosovo War of 1999 brought many new homeless people to Deponija, a Belgrade shanty town under the city's Pancevo Bridge. Despite plans to demolish this poor and unserviced settlement it remains home to thousands of Europeans.

Christiana, Copenhagen

A 'free town' within Copenhagen, Christiana is an alternative urban settlement nurtured within the confines of a former military barracks since 1971. Since then it has become one of the Danish city's most popular tourist attractions. Plans by politicians to 'normalise' Christiana continue to be rejected.

Developing World

Dharavi, Mumbai

Dharavi, a vast Mumbai slum, played a starring role in Danny Boyle's 2008 film *Slumdog Millionaire*. It is home to at least a million people, many engaged in the 'untouchable' tanning and leather industries. Although poor, this is a hardworking place peppered with 15,000 single-room factories.

The world's biggest shanty and slum towns are in the Indian subcontinent and Africa. Their scale is dumbfounding, and while plans do exist to improve many of them, corruption, bureaucracy, gang warfare and political ineptitude are just some of the barriers to progress. Another barrier is population growth, as if contraception has yet to be invented, although many people still believe their future welfare depends not on the state or local community but on having as many children as possible.

Orangi, Karachi (left)
Orangi is Asia's biggest slum. No one knows how many people live in this Karachi district, although censuses point to as many as 2.5 million. Although residents have made great strides in creating their own sewage system, Orangi, a haven for Islamic terrorists, is plagued by gang warfare.

Kya Sands, Johannesburg (right)
Industry has brought countless rural settlers to Johannesburg in search of jobs. When they have found work, they have often built their own makeshift homes near factories. Kya Sands might sound attractive, but this rough-and-ready settlement formed in the early 1990s is in need of basic services.

Kibera, Nairobi (left)
Kibera is Africa's biggest slum, but just part of a wider ring of shanty towns around Nairobi. Although running water has been installed, there is only one latrine for every fifty single-room shacks. These are emptied into the river. Unemployment stands at 50 per cent. Drugs and tainted alcohol are cheap.

Introduction

Many towns grew up around forts and castles. Others emerged from forts and castles. These are garrison towns, military settlements that have developed beyond strictly functional purposes and blurred the boundaries between military and civilian life. Some have evolved along impressive architectural lines and, when still under the auspices of the military, have maintained a purity of look and purpose denied to purely civilian towns that tend to change far more with the winds of trade and tides of fashion.

Fort George
Located on a promontory jutting into the Moray Firth, Fort George looks like some ideal 18th-century town. Wholly unspoilt, this star-pattern military garrison was built, to the designs of Colonel William Skinner and the Adam brothers, after the 1745 Jacobite uprising to pacify the Highlands of Scotland.

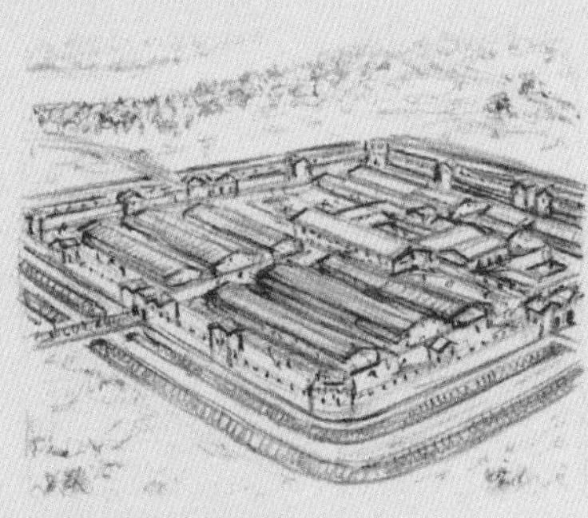

Roman garrisons

Roman military camps were towns in miniature laid out along geometric lines codified in pattern books. Foursquare, they featured simple grids of axial streets, running water, sanitation and heated buildings. Their plans can still be seen in Castres (France) and Marsala (Sicily).

Plaza del Cerro, Chimayo

To defend themselves from attack by American Indians, 18th-century Spanish settlers in New Mexico built settlements in the form of fortified squares. Based on Roman military camps, one at least survives – Plaza del Cerro, Chimayo – complete with a low-key yet exquisite church.

Camp Bastion

Measuring 6.4 km by 3.2 km (4 miles by 2 miles), Camp Bastion, Helmand Province, Afghanistan was designed and built by British military engineers to accommodate up to 28,000 troops and ancillary staff. The biggest British military base since the Second World War, it was handed to the Afghan National Army in 2014.

The Wolf's Lair, Rastenburg

An unintended model for the Brutalist architecture and planning of the 1960s, the Wolfsschanze (Wolf's Lair) was Adolf Hitler's Eastern Front command centre, a 6.5-sq km (2.5-sq mile) garrison secreted in the Masurian woods, East Prussia. Reinforced concrete bunkers, barracks and a cinema were scattered between trees.

Civilian Life

After serving 25 years, Roman soldiers retired on a pension. Many chose to remain with the armies that they knew so well, working at civilian trades within military garrisons. This marriage of military life and civilian trade evolved into major towns that, once dominated by armies, gradually found independent lives of their own. And, yet, the roots of these towns remain easy to identify. Fortifications aside, their streets are often lined with regular and even severe buildings, seemingly on parade.

Quebec
The only fortified American city north of Mexico, Quebec – founded by the French explorer and soldier Samuel de Champlain in 1608 – is a strategically located city noted for its defensive walls and 17th- and 18th-century cobbled streets lined with handsome houses and crowned with a lyrical skyline.

Londonderry

Despite the 105-day Siege of Derry by a Jacobite army in 1689, the 17th-century walls of Londonderry, Northern Ireland, have never been breached. The walls were built to defend English and Scottish settlers new to Ireland during the reign of King James I.

Clonmel

Clonmel was seized by Cromwell in 1650 and became an Irish garrison town. Its walls and barracks lent it a military air even in peacetime. The garrison was extended in 1805 when Napoleon threatened. Closed in 2012, plans for the future are under discussion.

Rabat

For the Berber emperor Abd al Mu'min, Rabat (Morocco) was the springboard for the invasion of the Iberian Peninsula. From 1146, he fortified the town, and although his imperial adventures ended in defeat, the stones of the Atlantic city still recall those heady days of Berber military expansion.

Mullingar

Mullingar, another Irish town characterised by its historic army barracks – closed in 2012 – is also defined by key buildings that, although designed for civilian life, have a distinctly military air about them. Belvedere House, a Palladian hunting lodge of 1740 looks ready to do battle.

Introduction

Venice
Venice is the most impressive and best-loved island city. An escape from Hunnish and other Dark Age invasions, it rose to become the seductive, if sometimes dark, heart of a mighty empire based on the strength of its navy and the acumen of its rulers and merchants.

'No man is an island/Entire of itself/Every man is a piece of the continent/A part of the main.' If you were to replace the word 'man' with the word 'city' in John Donne's 17th-century poem, you would not be wrong. Cities have been founded and have thrived on islands, yet they have rarely, if ever, been truly independent. Whether by ship, bridges or aircraft, island cities have been parts of much larger and more complex geographical and mercantile jigsaws.

Torcello (above)
In summer, the lagoon island of Torcello seems like a rural idyll especially after the exhausting experience of shoulder-rubbing Venetian alleys. And, yet, as the soaring early 11th-century campanile of its isolated and heartrending cathedral proves, this was once a densely populated city.

Venetian architecture (above)
The stones of Venice – its great basilica, cavernous churches, marble palaces – rise from wooden piles driven into the water that have turned into something like granite over generations. The city comprises 118 islands, served by 150 canals and linked by more than 400 bridges, one to the mainland.

Island life (below)
'I will arise and go now, and go to Innisfree/And a small cabin build there, of clay and wattles made.' In this poem of 1888, W. B. Yeats set up a lyrical tension between the grey trudge of city life and the rural idyll of life of an uninhabited island.

City of Amsterdam (below)
'God created the world, but the Dutch created Holland.' This saying recalls the inspired hydraulic engineering that enabled the Dutch to build on land – polder – reclaimed from marshes and the sea. Amsterdam became a city, *c.*1300, when a dam was built on the River Amstel to prevent flooding.

Major Cities

Venice Old City
St Mark's Square is symbolic of the civic grandeur of Venice – *La Serenissima* – at its political and mercantile zenith. Today, the population of the old city is 60,000, vastly outnumbered by that of day-tripping tourists. Most Venetians live and work in Mestre, an industrial suburb across the water.

While early island cities were often founded with defence uppermost in their citizens' minds, and although this continued to be a factor throughout history, later examples owe as much to their easy access to the sea and thus to both local and global trade. However, while there is something satisfying and even enchanting in the idea of a self-contained city, even the most successful of these has nearly always found it necessary to expand beyond its naturally prescribed limits.

Hong Kong

The population of Hong Kong was 3,000 when the British took control in 1842. Since then, this densely occupied island has become the dazzling hub of a city that, handed back to China in 1997, is nominally one of the world's wealthiest. The city stretches across the mainland today.

Florianopolis

Formerly Nossa Senhora do Desterro (Our Lady of Banishment), Florianopolis flourished in the 19th and 20th centuries with the arrival of immigrants from Germany and Italy. They added to the fascinating architectural and social mix of this thriving island city (pop: 500,000) in southern Brazil, famous for its 42 beaches.

Abu Dhabi

In the mid-20th century, Abu Dhabi's wealth was dependent on dates, pearls and camel herding. Oil was discovered in 1958. When the United Arab Emirates became independent in 1971, the island settlement on the Persian Gulf was transformed into a densely occupied, gridded, and extremely wealthy high-rise city.

Manhattan

Manhattan is perhaps the best known and most celebrated of all island cities. From the founding of the Dutch citadel of New Amsterdam in 1625, what became New York was settled incrementally until the entire island was one great maritime city. It has long since spread out to the mainland around it.

Island Towns

Lindau
Arriving by steamer, visitors to Lindau enter the Bavarian island town between a lighthouse and noble statue of a lion. Settled at first by nuns and then monks, Lindau became an Imperial Free City in 1275. Trade flourished. The town was connected to the mainland by railway in 1853.

Small islands have been settled by those seeking safety, religious seclusion or an escape from intolerance. Equally, they have served as ideal stopovers and refuelling points on trade routes. For these and other reasons, many evolved into flourishing towns, their size limiting overdevelopment. They tend to be characterised by dense street patterns and because of this they often eschew big modern buildings such as supermarkets and shopping centres: where these exist, they are often banished to the mainland.

Santa Elena & San Benito (right)

Linked by a causeway to the twin towns of Santa Elena and San Benito (Guatemala), Flores rises in a sea of red roofs, cobbled streets and Spanish colonial buildings from Lago Peten Itza. This was the last stronghold of the Mayans whose pyramids here were destroyed by the Spaniards.

Mexcaltitán (left)

A man-made island laid out as a symbol of the sun, Mexcaltitán (Mexico) is a small, as yet unspoilt shrimping town, that may well have been the original home of the Aztecs before they trekked north to found Tenochtitlan and their short-lived empire. It can only be reached by boat.

Trogir (right)

A Greek port on the Dalmatian coast from the 3rd century BCE, a refuge from Mongol hordes and nearly destroyed by Saracens, for centuries Trogir belonged to Venice. As a consequence, this island town, a part of Croatia today, has a remarkably rich heritage of Romanesque and early Renaissance buildings.

Introduction

Immediately after the attack on the twin towers of the World Trade Center on 11th September 2001, I was asked to write a 2,000-word newspaper article in response to the question posed by my editor: 'In the light of what's happened in New York, does the skyscraper have a future?' My initial response was that I needed just one word: 'Yes'. Since the first bricks of the first ziggurats were laid, humans have dreamed of building as high as the sky.

Sixth Avenue, New York
There are several reasons towns and cities have soared skywards. In ancient times, across cultures and through to the 19th century, this was usually in honour of gods. From then on, it was a question of space: the only way to create bigger buildings as here in Manhattan was upwards.

The original skyscrapers

Before the age of skyscrapers, the tallest buildings – rivalled only by the Great Pyramid of Cheops (139 m/455 ft) – were Europe's medieval cathedrals. When these were clustered round with parish churches sporting spires, as was old St Paul's, London, the effect was like a soaring forest of sculpted stone.

San Gimignano

In certain lights the 13th- and 14th-century tower houses of San Gimignano (Tuscany) might be mistaken for either giant termites' nests or a medieval Manhattan. Rising as high as 70 m (230 ft), there were 72 of these defensive tower houses before Black Death blighted the town in 1328.

Termite towers

Before humans began to build, termites in Africa, Australia and South America created, as they continue to do, mud nests rising more than 12-m (40-ft) high. Inside, these towering and ingeniously ventilated nests resemble densely occupied cities: early humans must have looked at them in awe. Could they build so high?

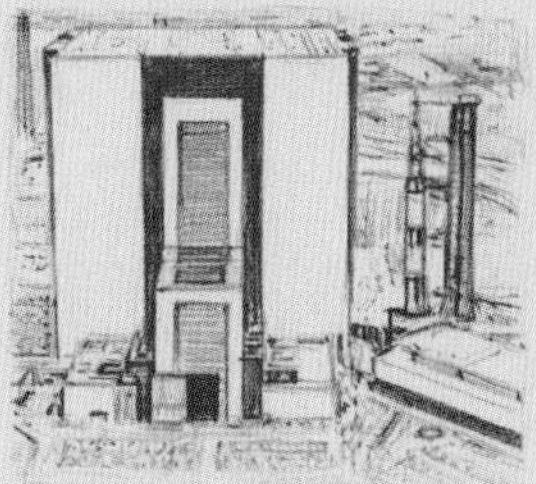

Cape Kennedy launch pad

One logical extension of building so very high was to leave the Earth. In 1969, the Apollo space programme took Neil Armstrong and Buzz Aldrin to the Moon. Their Saturn V rocket was built in the 160-m (526-ft) high Vertical Assembly Building at NASA's Kennedy Space Center, Florida.

Europe

Cologne Cathedral
Holy relics could make the fortunes of medieval cathedrals and their attendant cities. When the Holy Roman Emperor Frederick Barbarossa brought those of the Three Kings to Cologne, a vast cathedral was built to house them. Began in 1248 and completed in 1880, Cologne cathedral rises 157-m (515-ft) above the Rhine.

Greek and Roman cities were low lying. There had been little attempt to rise heavenwards as was common in cultures beyond the Mediterranean. A combination of ambition, rivalry and a vigorous display of devotion encouraged medieval Roman Catholic bishops to egg their masons into building as high as possible. If buildings collapsed in the process, this was simply encouragement to try again, and even higher. Soaring spires made it clear that God and religion were the core of city life.

Frankfurt rebuilt

Ravaged by Allied bombing, from 1945 Frankfurt (Germany) was rebuilt on determinedly modern lines. Nicknamed 'Mainhattan' – it stands on the River Main – and 'Chicago-am-Main' its many office towers rise from the city centre, itself unlike many other European cities where skyscrapers tend to be clustered on the edge.

International Business Centre, Moscow

Today, many European cathedrals, no matter how high, are being dwarfed by ever taller, ever more flamboyant towers devoted to the worship of Mammon rather than God. Moscow's International Business Centre is 2.5 km (1.5 miles) west of Red Square, but, with a plethora of extremely tall towers, it makes its presence felt.

Canary Wharf, London

A US-style city seemingly detached from the rest of London, although linked by public transport, Canary Wharf is a concatenation of office towers on the site of the former West India Dock, closed in 1980. A rival financial centre to the City of London, Canary Wharf continues to expand eastwards.

La Défense, Paris

Sited at the western end of the 10-km (6.2-mile) axis leading inexorably from the Louvre along the Champs Élysées, through the Arc de Triomphe and down the Avenue de la Grande Armée, La Défense is a defiantly modern business district of Paris created in 1958 and crowded with office towers.

Worldwide

The modern skyscraper emerged from the sidewalks of US cities in the last quarter of the 19th century. The invention of reliable steel and the elevator at the same time as Chicago and New York boomed sent these cities skywards. A combination of upward pressure on land prices and prestige encouraged ever taller buildings. The same factors, together with a copycat spirit, saw skyscrapers rising across the United States and, within a remarkably short space of time, around the world.

Pittsburgh
Pittsburgh, a steel city, was a natural home for the skyscraper, and so much so that in 1934, the world's first educational high-rise building was completed in this city. This is the University of Pittsburgh's Cathedral of Learning, an astonishing 163-m (535-ft) Neo-Gothic tower, which was designed by Charles Klauder, combining medieval and modern construction.

Mumbai

Home of Bollywood as well as high-tech enterprises, Mumbai (also known as Bombay) is India's wealthiest, most overtly glamorous and most dynamic city. From making its living through fishing, textiles and shipping, it entered the 21st century at lightning speed and with dozens of skyscrapers.

Victoria Harbour

Hong Kong's Victoria Harbour boasts one of the world's most compelling skylines. Today, the Chinese city has more skyscrapers – buildings over 150 m (492 ft) – than any other in the world. When Kai Tak Airport closed in 1998, the lifting of height restrictions led to further boom in high-rise buildings.

São Paulo

Founded as a Jesuit mission in 1554, São Paulo is the financial and industrial centre of Brazil today, its population density six times greater than that of Chicago – a fact that can be verified by looking out of any high downtown window at the surrounding walls of tall buildings.

Shanghai

Shanghai subsidised the Chinese government for several decades until economic reform in 1991 allowed this most enterprising and energetic coastal city to race ahead financially. As it boomed, so it built hundreds of ambitious skyscrapers, mostly in Pudong, across the Huangpu River from the historic Bund area.

UNDERGROUND CITIES

Introduction

To sustain their carpets of streets and forests of buildings, cities are supported by underground worlds of railway lines, sewers, water mains, electricity ducts, gas pipes, telecommunication cables, road tunnels, bomb shelters, catacombs and secret rivers. What is remarkable is that a great many of these underground ventures have been driven through hard rock, soft clay or even crumbling sand. It seems astonishing that cities, like long-legged flies on water, are able to support themselves on such excavated foundations without sinking.

Mayakovksy Metro Station, Moscow
'*. . . It is essential/That every evening/At least one star should ascend/ Over the crest of a building.*' It seems odd, then, that the poet Vladimir Mayakovksy is commemorated in the design of a Moscow Metro station 33-m (108-ft) below ground. And yet, Mayakovskaya Station (1938) is deeply poetic.

Rotherhithe Tunnel, London

A new invention – the tunnelling shield by Marc Brunel and Thomas Cochrane – made it possible to construct the world's first tunnel under a navigable river. This was the Rotherhithe Tunnel, London (1843), designed by Brunel and his son, Isambard. Although used by pedestrians only, it paved the way for railway and road tunnels below city rivers.

Tube as shelter

During the Second World War, London was bombed heavily by aerial flotillas of German aircraft, flying bombs and ballistic missiles. More than 80,000 Londoners were killed or seriously injured and more than 100,000 homes destroyed. Deep below ground, the city's familiar Tube stations served as reliable bomb shelters.

Underground Paris

Much of Paris is built of stone excavated from beneath the city itself. By the late 18th century, the underground quarries were extensive, and from 1785 they were used as ossuaries, vast underground cemeteries, for corpses that could no longer fit in the compact city's churchyards.

Hyde Park corner subway, London

The 'comprehensive redevelopment' of cities like London in the 1960s was essentially a marriage of the needs of the car and property deals that destroyed countless old streets and historic buildings. To add insult to injury, pedestrians were forced below traffic in labyrinthine subways.

Industrial Troglodytes

Wieliczka salt mines, Krakow
The Wieliczka salt mines extend for 286 km (178 miles). They produced table salt from the 13th century until 2007. Visitors are astonished by underground Roman Catholic chapels carved from salt and lit by salt chandeliers.

Unknown to many citizens, certain cities contain vast underground complexes including living spaces. Some are historic – like catacombs and mines – while others date from the Cold War era and were largely secret until the fall of the Berlin Wall and the end of Communist rule in Eastern Europe and the Soviet Union. Because no one this side of Nostradamus can predict the future with any certainty, such spaces are unlikely to be given over wholly to new purposes.

Sonnenberg tunnel, Lucerne (right)
A law of 1963 promised every Swiss citizen protection from nuclear attack. The Sonnenberg tunnel (1971–76) on the A2 motorway at Lucerne promised shelter for 20,000 people. Huge doors would seal the tunnel – equipped with a hospital, command centre and radio studio – but few believed it would work.

La Ville Souterraine, Montreal (left)
The brainchild of Vincent Ponte, an urban planner, Montreal's La Ville Souterraine (Underground City) was created in 1963 and today extends to 32 km (20 miles) of passageways beneath the city. This allows people to walk in the bitterest winter days from Metro stations to shops, offices and home while keeping warm and dry.

The Underground Great Wall, Beijing (right)
In 1969, at the height of tensions between China and the Soviet Union, Mao Zedong ordered the construction of an enormous underground shelter in Beijing. Dug by hand by 300,000 citizens, including children, the labyrinth, known as the Underground Great Wall, included hospitals and theatres. It became a tourist attraction.

Introduction

Ancient Rome
All roads lead to Rome. What was also true is that roads led away from Rome, stretching out to 2,000 cities across the empire in the 3rd century CE. Every Roman citizen belonged to one of these cities, and they were all scions of the megalopolis of Rome itself.

Megalopolis was founded in 371 BCE by the Theban general Epaminondas after his victories over the Spartans. '*By my counsels was Sparta shorn of her glory/. . . By the arms of Thebes was Megalopolis encircled with walls/And all Greece won independence and freedom,*' boasted the legend on his tomb. The Spartans, however, got their own back and destroyed this large Greek city. Today, the term 'megalopolis' is used for cities – urban juggernauts – that have spread across entire regions.

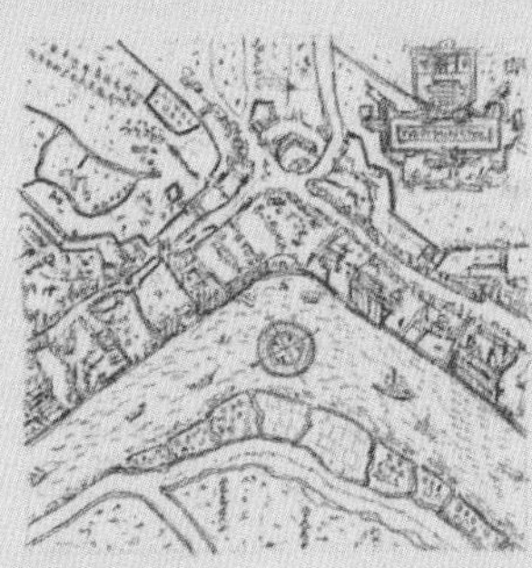

London's growth

London dates from 47 CE. The city expanded south to Southwark with the first London Bridge, and over the centuries joined hands with what, from the 11th century, had become the City of Westminster. Despite a mid-20th century 'Green Belt' intended to keep its girth in control, it continues to grow.

Canton

From the 18th century, London traded with China through the East India Company and Canton. Britain exchanged wool and cotton for tea, silk and porcelain. But, the lucrative export of opium upset the Chinese and led to the Opium Wars of 1840. The victorious British opened Canton to international trade.

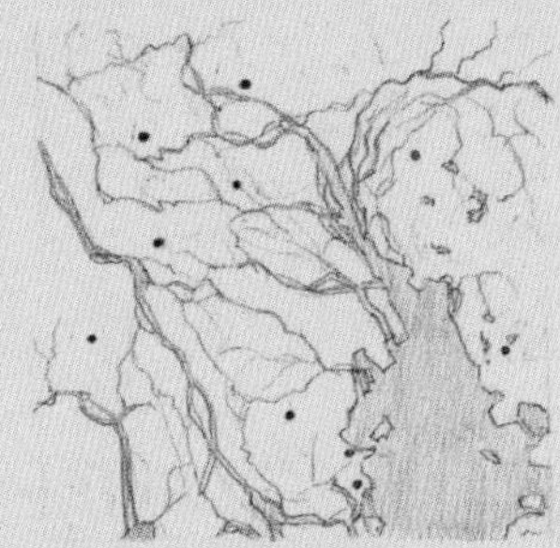

Pearl River Delta Mega City

Canton, now Guangzhou, has certainly prospered. Today, it is the centre of what is known as the Pearl River Delta Mega City, a gradual joining up of several old and new towns and cities, forming an economic powerhouse and a megalopolis of some 44 million people.

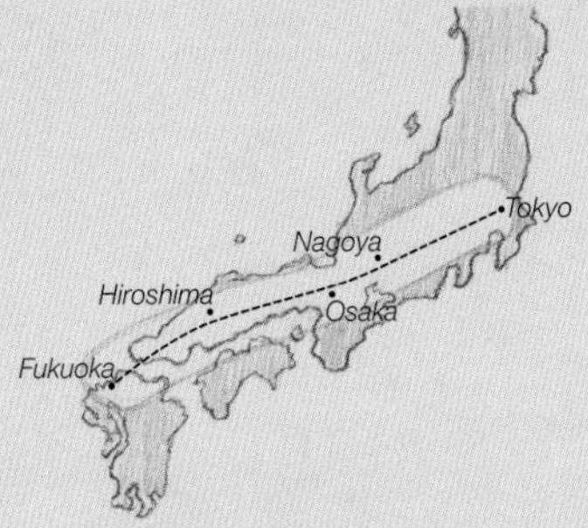

Taiheiyo Belt

Japan's Taiheiyo Belt or Tokaido Corridor is a 1,207-km (750-mile) stretch of almost continuous urban development from Mito to Fukuoka through Greater Tokyo and Osaka along high-speed railway and motorway routes. Not quite one big city, but evidence that cities are beginning to merge.

Europe's Mega Cities

London's motorways
As the economy of cities follow transport corridors, suburbia sprouts alongside with ever more low-rise housing, out-of-town shopping malls and leisure centres. In this sense the city tends to degrade while becoming too big to function sensibly or happily as traffic increases and commuting times lengthen.

The development of mega cities in Europe has followed railway and motorway corridors. Britain's 'Silicon Valley' courses along the Great Western Railway route from London to Bristol, shadowed by the M4 motorway. High-tech businesses developed along the 'valley', pulling towns and cities east and west. This phenomenon dates back even earlier to the age of canals, although cities along these industrial waterways saw themselves as rivals rather than as urban bedfellows. Dense regional transport networks, however, tend to blur civic identities.

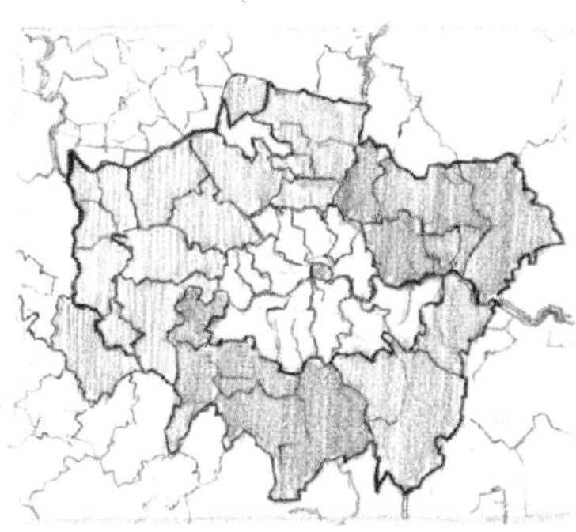

Greater London
As London grew and its suburbs spread it swallowed up not just old market farms and what had been remarkably rural villages until the early 1900s, but an entire county. In 1965 when the Greater London Council was formed, Middlesex all but disappeared off the map.

Liverpool and Manchester Railway
The Liverpool and Manchester Railway (1830) boosted trade between these two Lancashire cities. However, because Liverpool imposed heavy tariffs on goods by sea to Manchester, a ship canal was opened between this inland city and the sea in 1894. What could have been a successful partnership ended in regional rivalry.

The Rhine
The German economy, and that of some of its principal regions and cities, is aided immeasurably by the Rhine, a river navigable by ships and industrial barges for hundreds of miles. While cities along the Rhine maintain distinct identities, their economies are linked by this riverine corridor.

Dutch unity
Close together, Dutch cities are served by an efficient public transport network connecting trains, trams, buses and bicycles almost seamlessly. This makes it easy for people to work between cities. It is almost as if – and despite the manicured countryside between them – Dutch cities are a single entity.

Global Mega Cities

In 2015, 55 per cent of the world's population lived in cities, a figure that is expected to rise to as much as 75 per cent by 2030. Most of this urban growth will be in poorer countries as rural people continue to flock to cities in search of work and a better life. Equally, further development of transport corridors between cities in the developed world will catch people in the urban net even when they imagine themselves to be prosperous country folk.

Los Angeles
Los Angeles, a city owned by Spain and Mexico before becoming part of the US in 1850, offers precious little public transport. Measuring 71 km by 47 km (44 miles by 29 miles), it is a huge city with a population of 13 million (Greater Los Angeles). Traffic jams are a way of life.

Jakarta
The population of Jakarta (Indonesia) is eight million, of which four million commute each working day. Congestion has been appalling for years. The city's first Metro line is due to open in 2018. Meanwhile, a network of flyovers, under construction since 2010, will encourage even more cars.

São Paulo
A curious feature of most American cities and the link between them is a paucity of railways. Cars and roads pre-dominate. In São Paulo, roads that seem fast on a road engineer's plan are quite the opposite. There are so many cars that their use is rationed.

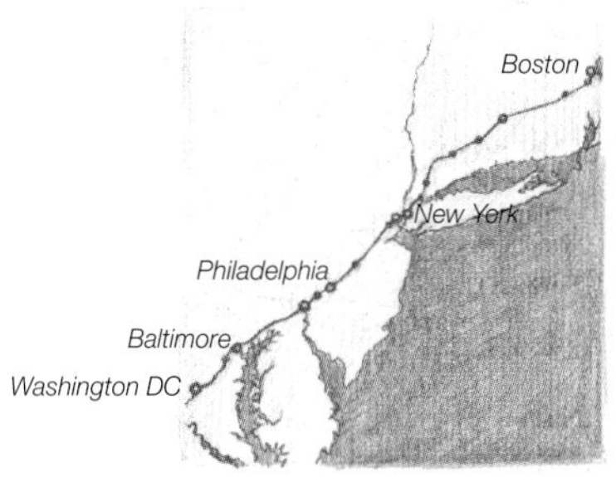

North East Corridor
The North East Corridor of the United States from Boston to Washington DC via New York, Philadelphia and Baltimore is an economic powerhouse served, unlike the rest of the US, by high-speed electric trains. Major investment from 2010 will see train times cut by almost half by 2040.

Merging Cities
Cities set very close together have sometimes merged completely like Buda and Pest (Hungary). Others known as twin cities, like Minneapolis and St Paul, Minnesota, maintain separate identities and have often duplicated city services unnecessarily rather than combine efforts. Long-distance road signs, however, lump the twins together.

Introduction

Letchworth
The first 'Garden City' was a new town, Letchworth, 64 km (40 miles) north of London. Designed in an Arts and Craft style, it began life as an upright, abstemious community. Londoners would come up for the day on cheap excursions from King's Cross to gawp at the 'Garden City' folk.

The Garden City movement, created by the Victorian social reformer Ebenezer Howard, looked forward to the day when honest, decent people might live in new towns that combined the best of urban and rural ways. While living in the United States, Howard was influenced by the works of the poet Walt Whitman and essayist Ralph Waldo Emerson and their pleas for a romantic individualism. Such was the life to be led in garden cities beyond the long shadow of London.

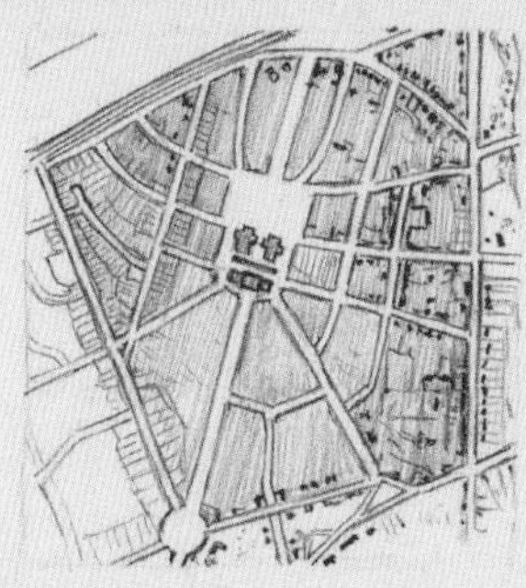

Letchworth plan

Raymond Unwin and Barry Parker's 1904 plan for Letchworth depicted avenues radiating from a central square to village greens. Writer Walter Wilkinson thought Letchworth preachy: *'It's lectures, lectures all day long/And lectures all night too!/ They've all of 'em got their opinions/And all their opinions is new.'*

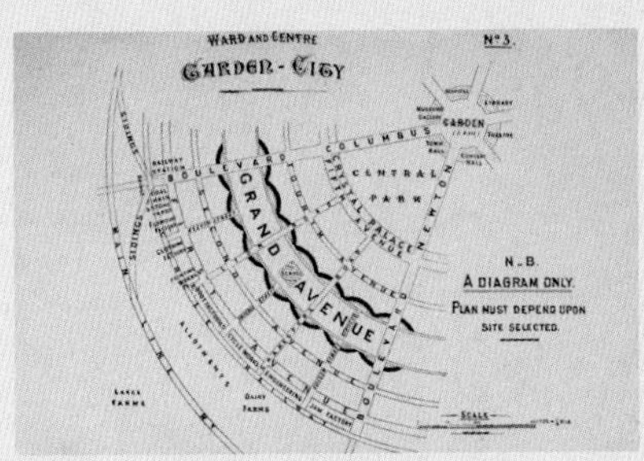

Garden city plan

Ebenezer Howard's own plans for ideal Garden Cities were more concerned with the big picture than with the kind of loving detail put into practice by Unwin and Parker. His geometric diagrams illustrate small, self-sufficient cities with central areas encircled by allotments, orchards, farms and smallholdings.

Arts and Crafts cottages

Raymond Unwin joined William Morris's Socialist League in 1885. With Barry Parker he wrote *The Art of Building a Home* (1901). Letchworth's cottages reflected their ideals. In such homes, the poet John Betjeman teased, *'Sympathy is stencilling/Her decorative leatherwork/Wilfred's learned a folk-tune for/The Morris Dancers' band.'*

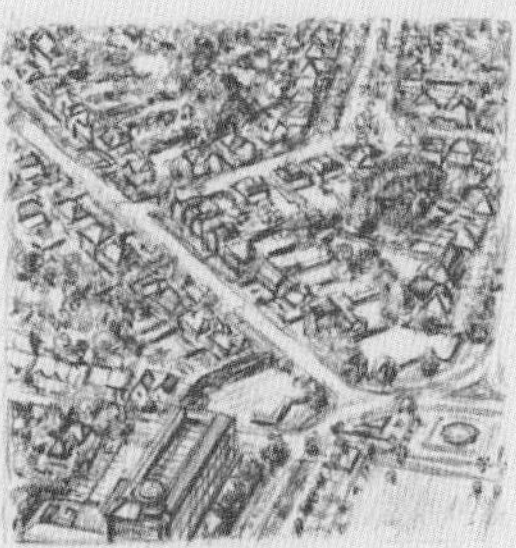

100 years of green

Letchworth celebrated its centenary in 2003. It had evolved more or less successfully, a green town with a population of 32,000. Its Arts and Crafts architecture had stood up well. What it was not, though, was self-sufficient. Instead of smallholders and 'stencillers', it had largely become a commuter town.

Growth of the Garden City Movement

Welwyn Garden City
Ebenezer Howard's Neo-Georgian style Welwyn Garden City, 32 km (20 miles) north of London dates from 1920. Howard's belief in public ownership meant that, at first, there was only one shop providing everything a citizen required. He would not have understood consumerism.

In the 1900s, England was a test bed for new ideas in social housing and town planning. Eminent European architects, politicians, planners and theorists came to see the new garden cities and suburbs. They were impressed and took away many of Ebenezer Howard's ideas, as well as Arts and Crafts architecture and design, reproducing these in fresh ways, notably in Germany and Austria. At the time, industrial cities seemed so irredeemably unsanitary that building anew seemed the best way forward.

Hampstead Garden City (right)
Hampstead Garden City was never a home to all social classes as planned. In stark contrast, Teutoburgia (1909–23) was designed as a Garden City for German miners of the Ruhr town, Herne. Its 530 English-style Arts and Crafts homes and gardens are now a sanctuary for the German middle classes.

Austrian garden cities (left)
Garden suburbs such as Hietzing and Döbling are notable features of the outer rings of Vienna. Developed from the 1860s with the building of comfortable villas for the industrial middle class, from 1900 until the late 1920s, they were repeated on a more modest scale for working-class families, too.

Hellerau, Dresden (right)
The first German Garden City was Hellerau (1909), Dresden, funded by the furniture manufacturer Karl Schmidt-Hellerau. Its Arts and Crafts cottages were designed by, among other distinguished architects, Hermann Muthesius, author of a three-volume report *Das englische Haus* (1904–05), a comprehensive study of English Arts and Crafts domestic design.

New Town Movement

Harlow shopping centre
Architectural fanfares for the common man, New Towns were to be English society's level playing fields, free of class distinction, public schools and dirty drains. But, not even a Lynn Chadwick sculpture on the facade of a shopping centre could attract the middle classes.

The New Town Act of 1946 decreed the creation of 11 English New Towns. Most of these were 'overspill' towns, an attempt to solve London's housing crisis immediately after the Second World War when so many homes had been destroyed. They were also to be places where, according to Lewis Silkin, minister of town and country planning in Britain's post-war Labour government, 'all classes of community can meet freely together on equal terms and enjoy common cultural and recreational facilities.'

Harlow

Time passed all too slowly for many 1950s housewives exiled from scruffy, yet bustling London streets to houses in Harlow or other New Towns, which, although clean and new, were located a long walk from new shopping centres. 'New Town Blues' was the sorry order of the day.

Basildon

'Basildon', said Lewis Silkin, 'will become a city which people from all over the world will want to visit.' Despite its trim modern architecture, by Frederick Gibberd, who went on to design Liverpool's Roman Catholic cathedral, the tourists never came in anything other than dribs and drabs.

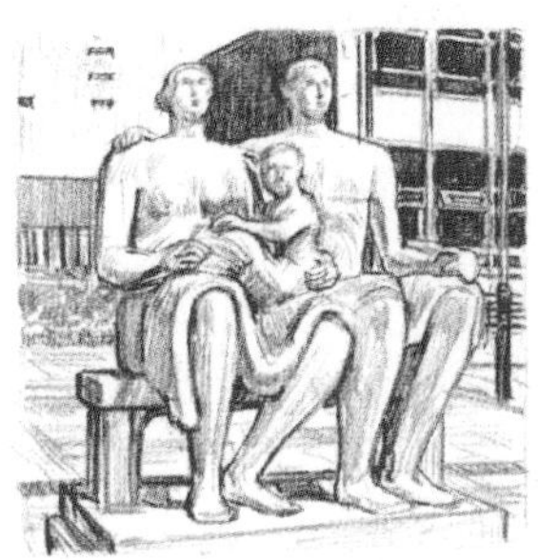

***The Family*, Harlow**

Art, it was believed, would inspire the 1.5 million Londoners moving to New Towns. In 1956, Sir Kenneth Clark, the patrician arts grandee, unveiled Henry Moore's *The Family* in Harlow, congratulating the London diaspora for 'making a work of art a focal centre of a new town'.

Crawley

Art came late to Crawley, yet what this New Town had was Gatwick, which from 1950 was designated London's second airport. This encouraged a boom in light manufacturing and service industries. While Crawley cannot be called attractive from an aesthetic viewpoint, it has never lacked jobs.

New Towns Expansion

Milton Keynes
Derek Walker, the young chief architect and planner of Milton Keynes, wanted this latest New Town to be more in tune with nature than its smaller, older siblings. Millions of trees were planted, while a total of 20 per cent of the town was given over to parkland.

The first 11 New Towns lacked social diversity. They offered little in the way of the excitement of cities or the charms of traditional towns. When Milton Keynes, a much bigger proposition of 250,000 people was planned in the 1960s, these problems were to be addressed. Yet, because the car was king in that decade of triumphant technological progress, Milton Keynes was laid out on a free-flowing grid of dual carriageways as if the car had usurped the citizen.

Cumbernauld

Could an entire New Town be housed in one single concrete megastructure? Could pedestrians and cars be separated from one another completely? These are questions the architects of Cumbernauld, a Glasgow overspill town created in 1955, set out to answer under the leadership of Dudley Roberts Leaker with unique results.

Stevenage

Stevenage New Town boasts Britain's first purpose-built traffic-free shopping zone, opened by Queen Elizabeth in 1959. By the time it needed remodelling in the 21st century, funds and enthusiasm were hard to come; by now, the New Towns been taken out of the hands of paternalistic development corporations.

Peterlee

Peterlee, a New Town for coal miners in County Durham, was to have been a celebration of high-rise architecture by the radical, Georgian-born architect Berthold Lubetkin. Poor new housing was built instead, but with the soaring ambition of Lubetkin's vision encapsulated in Victor Pasmore's Apollo Pavilion of 1969.

Church of Christ the Cornerstone, Milton Keynes

The domed Church of Christ the Cornerstone (Ian Smith, 1991) was the first ecumenical town-centre church built in Britain. It was a well-intended manifestation of the idea that New Towns were open to everyone and free from old dogmas, prejudices and downright vicious religions.

Global New Towns

St Quentin-en-Yvelines
At the uncertain heart of St Quentin-en-Yvelines, one of five Parisian new towns dating from the 1960s, is a rectangular lake flanked and partly crossed by three mighty and either gloriously or insanely over-the-top Postmodern Classical housing blocks designed by Ricardo Bofill's Taller de Arquitectura.

As cities burst at the seams from the mid-1950s, they could either expand in random fashion or build rigorously planned New Towns, or satellite towns. While the majority of these around the world have been, at best, lacklustre, there have been attempts, notably in France and China, to create something quite new: satellite and new towns on an epic scale with surprising architecture and unexpected urban planning to match. However controversial, these offer some sort of riposte to unmitigated sprawl.

Marne-la-Vallée

Marne-la-Vallée, another Parisian New Town, is characterised by outlandish architecture, too. Les Arènes de Picasso (1980–84) provides 540 apartments in a sensational building – part Art Deco, part Gaudí, part concrete megastructure – by Manuel Nunez Yanowsky, a former partner of Ricardo Bofill in Barcelona.

Eurodisney

Given the cinematic nature of some of Marne-la-Vallée's architecture, it seems appropriate that the new town is also home to Eurodisney where you can stay in themed hotels, taking you from urban deprivation and sprawl to the worlds of New York, Santa Fe and Davy Crockett.

Parisian sprawl

Despite the efforts of architects like Ricardo Bofill to imbue these Parisian new towns with a sense of identity and history, they have been allowed to sprawl along RER suburban railway lines with little attempt to cluster them around central cores. For many residents they are modern ghettoes.

Les Espaces D'Abraxas

Les Espaces D'Abraxas (1978–84) at Marne-la-Vallée comprise L'Arc, Le Théâtre and Le Palacio, three spectacular prefabricated concrete postmodern Classical housing blocks that possibly give residents of this new town a sense that they are today's Romans.

Replicas

Tianducheng
A one-third-scale replica of the Eiffel Tower soars, as best as it can, over the mansard roofs of Haussmann-era Parisian avenues and over gardens mimicking those of Versailles. This is Tianducheng (2007), a gated 'new town' 40 minutes drive from Hangzhou, China's fourth largest city.

For some Chinese people who have lived for decades in grim state-approved concrete housing blocks, a chance to live at home yet in France, England or Italy at the same time is a dream come true. In recent years replica European cities have sprung up in China. To Western eyes, they are bizarre, emerging from paddy fields alongside new motorways. These are not exactly new towns, but gated housing estates set too far from existing cities for comfort or convenience.

Thames Town, Songjiang New City
Thames Town (Atkins, 2006) is far from London. 32 km (20 miles) from Shanghai. It is a colourful Chinese interpretation of an English country town and bits of London, watched over by statues of Winston Churchill and Harry Potter. Popular as a wedding venue, it has been less successful in attracting residents.

Huangzhou's Venetian water town
Gondolas ply the canals of Huangzhou's Venice water town. With a Metro station, it is more successful than other ersatz European towns. Life here, though, is not exactly Venetian: St Mark's Square features a baseball court, while workers from a nearby amusement park sleep in dormitories in the Doge's Palace.

Seaside, Florida
Seaside is a re-imagining of an old-fashioned Florida seaside resort. Built on land owned by Robert S. Davis who toured old towns with a group of New Urbanist architects to study vernacular buildings, contemporary architects working in a variety of pseudo-historic styles have added to the town's gaiety.

Celebration, Florida
Like a set design for *The Stepford Wives*, Celebration, Florida, is a younger sibling of Seaside. Developed by the Walt Disney Company from 1994, it was master-planned by Robert A. M. Stern and Cooper, Robertson and Partners. There is fake snow in the town square at Christmas.

Introduction

St James's Park, London
One of the most compelling vistas of any city is the view of government buildings at the east end of the lake in London's St James's Park. Trees reflected in water frame what appears to be some fairy-tale palace, an optical illusion through which several buildings meld into one.

Trees transform towns and cities. They bring colour, shade and wildlife to the busiest streets: Grand avenues lined with trees sometimes as far as the eye can see; London's garden squares; Tokyo's cherry blossom; roads lined with poplars leading inexorably to the heart of provincial French towns. Working hand-in-frond with nature, these are some of the high points of urban planning. The power of trees to transform the hottest, driest, dustiest streets in a city is the stuff of elemental sorcery.

French provincial towns

When French country lanes turn into avenues of tall trees, travellers sense that they must be nearing a town. Usually, they are. The device is a powerful one, directing attention and traffic to the heart of provincial towns, with the trees gradually giving way to brick, stone and timber buildings.

Cherry blossom, Kakunodate

Cherry trees blossom throughout Japan. One of the most exquisite walks in any Japanese town in April is the 2 km (1.2 miles) path along the Hinokinai River in Kakunodate, Akita Province. The blossom of the weeping cherry trees contrasts with dark walls of a wealth of historic samurai houses.

Holland Park Avenue, London

On a grand scale, Holland Park Avenue is an ancient British track transformed into a Roman road and, in the early to mid-19th century, one of London's busiest yet most handsome major streets. Giant plane trees line this expensive thoroughfare from Notting Hill Gate to the Holland Park roundabout.

Pennsylvanian Amish

Amish buggies ambling along avenues of tall, shady trees into Pennsylvanian towns with characterful names like Bird-in-Hand, Intercourse and Paradise, are a dreamlike counterbalance to the sight of cars thundering along busy streets rolling into US towns past shopping malls and loud roadside adverts.

Eco Towns

Vauban, Freiburg
The Eco Town movement envisaged tidy minded citizens working to a close set of mutually agreed rules – environmental, social, architectural – guaranteeing a low-energy way of life. Founded in the mid-1990s on a former military base near Freiburg, Vauban, is a much-vaunted example of the type.

Most ancient towns were 'eco towns' in the sense that they used little in the way of natural resources compared to their successors. Man-made pollution was minimal and towns existed more or less in tune with nature. However, it also true that the building of towns from the era of Roman expansion onwards demanded the destruction of huge areas of what were once forests. Ever since, the relentless quest for urbanisation has set humankind at odds with the natural world. Today the big question is whether or not we can truly square environmental concerns with urban life.

Vathorst, Amersfoort (left)
Vathorst (West 8, 1996–2002) is a free-standing extension of Amersfoort, a low-density yet compact new town on the edge of an existing historic town, offering commerce, industry and high-quality social housing: it offers a far more sustainable way of urban development than suburbia.

Nieuwland, Amersfoort (right)
Nieuwland is an 'eco' suburb of Amersfoort, a Dutch town with a fine medieval centre. Five thousand low-rise homes were built between 1995 and 2002, designed to make as much use of solar energy as possible. These feed surplus energy into Holland's national grid.

Bicester (left)
Britain's contribution to the 'eco town' movement was a political gimmick announced in 2007 by a New Labour government. Unlike Vathorst, it envisaged a rash of developer-led, car-based suburban towns with tokenistic green credentials. Bicester, Oxfordshire, offers an 'eco pub' presumably for the sale of Greene King beer.

Eco Cities

Masdar City pod
Visitors to Masdar City, Abu Dhabi, are taken below ground by egg-like electric pods to central areas of this intriguing new settlement. Although these will not extend to the entire desert city when completed in 2025, they offer a glimpse of how cars can be replaced in Gulf cities.

Hundreds of years ago, Arabic merchants built beautiful houses tucked into the tight weave of medieval Cairo. With their cool courtyards, screens and rooftop wind towers drawing warm air up and away from shaded rooms, those that survive remain intoxicatingly beautiful as well as offering models of environmentally friendly design. The expansion and creation of brand new cities in the blazing heat of the Middle East has prompted politicians, architects and planners to think of both new and traditional ways of designing low-energy cities.

Masdar City central square (left)

In Masdar City's central square, a 45-m (148-ft) high wind tower, based on medieval principles, lifts warm air away from streets and brings cooling breezes in return. Terracotta-faced buildings lining the streets are a fusion of contemporary and historic design. A Metro link will connect Masdar City to Abu Dhabi.

Benidorm (right)

Until the advent of package holidays in the 1960s, Benidorm was an Andalucian fishing village. Today it has more high-rise buildings per capita than any other city. From 1985, Ricardo Bofill's neo-classical Parque de l'Aigüera has brought greenery and a sense of environmental responsibility to this overdeveloped Spanish holiday town.

Vitoria-Gasteiz (left)

The Basque city Vitoria-Gasteiz has greened itself with new tramways, cycle paths and avenues, and with the spectacular Palacio de Congresos (Urbanarbolismo and Unusualgreen, 2013), its walls alive with 33,000 species of indigenous plants, along with birds and butterflies. This is a showcase for green urban design.

Introduction

Petra
Petra (Jordan), the 'rose-red city half as old as time', was founded by the Nabateans in *c.*312 BCE and largely abandoned in a period of earthquakes around 106 CE. Home to 30,000 people, it was hidden in the recesses of mountains, its magical rock-cut buildings approached through a narrow defile.

Cities are as much organisms as they are rational constructs. They are born. They thrive, decline and die. Some of history's most ambitious cities were abandoned soon after they were built while others renew themselves over thousands of years. There are many reasons why cities fail to take root, among them insufficient water, political upheavals, earthquakes, tsunamis and rapid economic decline. And, yet, when there is the will, aqueducts can bring water and entire cities rebuilt after storms and war.

Pharaoh Akhenaten
The Pharaoh Akhenaten, husband of Nefertiti and father of Tutankhamun, decreed a new religion for Egypt and a new city where a single sky or sun god would be worshipped. After so many centuries of elaborate polytheism, this radical move made Akhenaten unpopular with priests and his subjects alike.

Amarna
Akhenaten's new city, Amarna, set more or less halfway along the Nile between Cairo and Luxor was built within just five years (1346–1341 BCE), most of its buildings made of whitewashed mud bricks. It was abandoned shortly after the Pharaoh's death when Tutankhamun returned to Thebes and the old religion.

Hatra
For centuries, the ruins of Hatra (Iraq), a Seleucid city founded in the 3rd century BCE, and capital of the first Arab kingdom, dazzled travellers with their architectural wealth. The Romans failed to destroy this temple-rich city. In 2015, vicious religious zealots razed this World Heritage Site.

Babylon
'This was built by Saddam Hussein, son of Nebuchadnezzar, to glorify Iraq' is an inscription once found on many of the bricks of the legendary city built, conquered, rebuilt and re-conquered many times in its long history. US forces damaged the abandoned city during the Gulf Wars.

Middle East & Central Asia

Ani

The 'City of 1001 churches', Ani (Turkey) was a fine Armenian city. Savaged by Turks in 1064, its ruins were to have been 'wiped off the face of the earth' by the Turkish army in 1921. General Kazim Karabekir refused, yet what survives is cruelly neglected.

Wondrous and heavily populated cities rose in the Middle East and across Central Asia over thousands of years. There may well be more to uncover in future, but this has long been a vast region of the world where warring dynasties have fought for space and, in the process and often as a matter of policy, have destroyed the cities they have conquered along with their populations. If you are lucky enough to have visited such cities, cherish their memories.

Persepolis

Darius I and Xerxes the Great built Persepolis (Iran) on an epic scale, and with eclectic, colourful architecture reflecting the breadth and depth of the Persian Empire. Alexander the Great torched this imposing city in 330 BCE. It limped on for another thousand years before succumbing to ruination.

Urgench

For centuries Urgench (Turkmenistan) founded in the 4th century was a proud medieval Silk Road city. Ravaged by Genghis Khan in 1221 and again by Timur (Tamerlane) in the late 14th century, it was finally abandoned when the Amu Darya River changed course, leaving it high, battered and dry.

Ctesiphon

From antiquity, Ctesiphon (Iraq) rose and fell and was moved several times. Between 570 and 637 CE, however, it was the world's largest city. The Muslim conquest of 637, however, led to the abandonment of the city as the new city of Baghdad, built from the stones of Ctesiphon, replaced it.

Hattusa

Hattusa (Turkey) was the capital of the Hittite Empire, reaching its zenith during the reign of Suppiluliuma I (1334–1322 BCE) who conquered Egyptian territories in Syria during the time of Pharaoh Akhenaten. Around 1200 BCE, the city was destroyed most probably by Kaskians from Anatolia and Phrygians from the southern Balkans.

Modern Cities

Hiroshima
On 6th August 1945, an atomic bomb dropped on Hiroshima from the US *Enola Gay*, killing 80,000 people in the industrial Japanese port city. A further 80,000 died of nuclear injuries. Seventy per cent of the city's buildings were destroyed. A deadly typhoon followed in September.

Earthquakes. Tsunamis. Warfare. Nuclear disasters. Modern cities can vanish off the face of the earth or lose their populations in an instant. Despite modern technology, the human need to destroy as well the vagaries of the Earth's behaviour – it, too, is an organism, and not some machine for living on – conspire to make cities less safe than their monumental construction suggests. Remarkably, though, and like fresh green shoots that emerge after a forest fire, cities are able to regenerate themselves.

Chernobyl (right)

On 26th April 1986, the Chernobyl nuclear power plant blew up, releasing radioactive particles across the USSR. Pripyat, dating from 1970, had been built to support the plant. At the time of the accident, its population of the Ukranian town was 50,000. Pripyat was abandoned on 28th April 1986.

Slavutych (left)

Slavutych was built east of Pripyat to replace the radioactive town. Two metres (6½ ft) of uncontaminated soil were spread across the site before building work began. Planted with trees and green spaces, Slavutych was to be a more pleasant town than Pripyat, although residents continue to leave to forget Chernobyl.

Banda Aceh (right)

The Indian Ocean tsunami of 2004 killed 167,000 people in the Indonesian city of Banda Aceh from a population of 240,000. Sixty per cent of its buildings were destroyed. And, yet, like villages, towns and cities elsewhere along Indian Ocean coasts, Banda Aceh has been rebuilt.

Introduction

Mega city
The Italian architect Paolo Soleri (1919–2013) imagined spectacular mega cities based on the principle of 'arcology' (architecture + ecology). Some were more overtly technological than others. The idea was to create cities of hundreds of thousands of people in mountainous geological structures that would leave much of the planet to nature.

Humans have long dreamed of heavenly cities, of New Jerusalems, castles in the sky, utopias and, from the late 19th centuries, cities in space. Rapid technological innovation encouraged inventors, novelists, engineers, scientists, artists and architects to dream up futuristic cities on earth, too. These were often concerned with speed, height and a very particular and ordered view of efficiency – relentless, fast, uniform and perhaps just a little inhuman. It is fascinating how so many resembled clusters of hi-tech termites' nests.

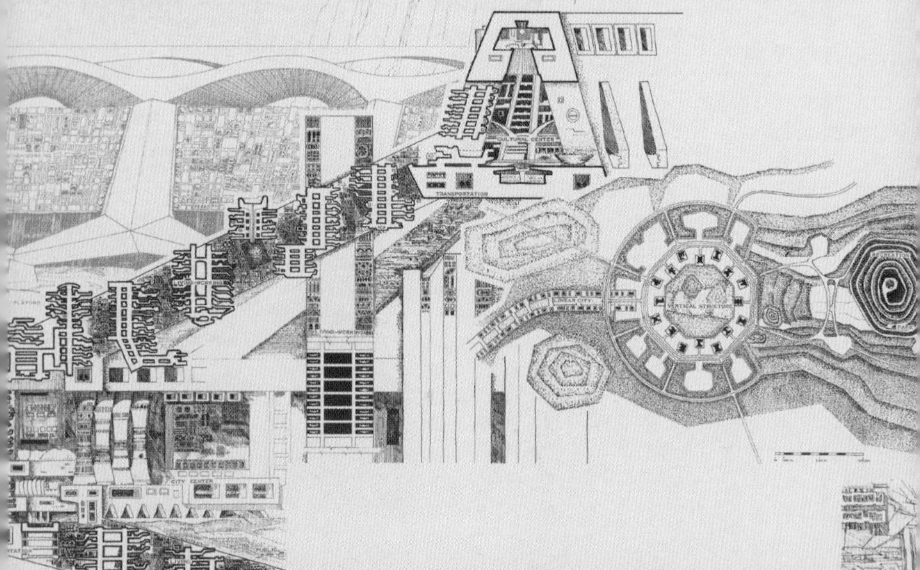

City of the Future

The sheer difficulty of getting about major 20th-century cities prompted architects and other visionaries to imagine the city of the future as a complex transport system moving people as quickly as possible from one Neo-Renaissance to the next. This is H. W. Corbett's *City of the Future* (1913).

Metropolis

Fritz Lang's German Expressionist masterpiece *Metropolis* (1927) presented cinema audiences with a brilliantly realised dystopian city of the future. The ruling class lived in high, magnificent modern accommodation, while the working class toiled in underground furnaces and machine rooms.

Jetpacks

One way to beat congestion, or so it seemed, to rocket scientists and comic-book artists, was to fly above cities using personal jetpacks. Developed from 1920, it was the operational Bell Rocket Belt of 1962 that truly caught the public imagination. Jetpacks, however, have yet to catch on.

Future colonies

Space colonies, or giant cities ferrying humans away from a polluted, violent earth to the stars, have been a perennial feature of science-fiction novels since the 1920s. In 1974, Gerard K. O'Neill, a US physicist, proposed a 32-km (20-mile) long cylindrical colony, assembled in space, for 'several million people'.

To Space & Back to Earth

Montreal Biosphere
The 62-m (203-ft) high Montreal Biosphere designed by Buckminster Fuller was originally the US Pavilion at Expo 67, a world exhibition that stirred the imaginations of hi-tech architects and designers. A much bigger geodesic dome could even house an entire city.

Space travel and new technologies associated with it encouraged ideas for cities in space and for science-fiction-style cities on earth. Yet, towns and cities continue to develop in earthly ways. This is not just because the majority of humans prefer to remain on earth, but also because new communications and other computer technologies developed during the era of Lunar rocketry have given world cities an all but invisible Space Age makeover.

Invisible wiring (left)
The all but secret nature of new communication technologies means that it is now possible to wire cities in ever more discreet ways. Together with less intrusive pipes, ducts and wires and serious attempts at energy and architectural conservation, a city of the future might look like a Canaletto painting.

Technology in Seoul (right)
By 2015, Seoul, with a population of 20 million, claimed to be the world's most 'wired' city, with Wi-Fi covering the entire metropolis. This has revolutionised city services and ways people live. Seoul made a conscious effort from 1997 onwards to shift from heavy industry to an info-tech-based economy.

Lunar base (left)
There is a very long way to go before cities on other planets become remotely real. Foster + Partners, however, are working with the European Space Agency on the development of robotic 3-D printing machines to build shelters and settlements from lunar dust on the Moon.

APPENDICES

Glossary

ACROPOLIS High, fortified area of ancient Greek city

AGORA Central marketplace (Ancient Greece)

ALLEY Passageway between buildings

AMPHITHEATRE Circular or oval open building for drama, sports and thrills (Greek and Roman)

ARCADE Colonnaded passageway, often with shops

AVENUE Broad thoroughfare lined with trees

AXIAL PLAN Geometric street layout linking places in straight lines

BAROQUE Theatrical style of 17th and early 18th centuries

BASILICA Oblong Roman law courts and assembly halls; churches in early Christian era

BLOCK Area of town or city framed by streets

BOOMTOWN Town experiencing rapid economic expansion

BOURSE Stock market; heart of financial districts

BOROUGH Administrative district of a town or city

BOROUGH SURVEYOR Key urban planning official especially in the 19th and 20th centuries

BOULEVARD Wide street or avenue, long associated with 'flâneurs'

BREAD AND CIRCUSES Ancient Roman policy of keeping citizens passive with free food and cheap, mass entertainment; familiar today

BROWNFIELD SITE Disused urban area rife for redevelopment

CEMETERY Public burial ground

CIRCUS Circular road met by converging streets

CITADEL Fortress commanding a city from on high

CITIZEN Inhabitant of a town or city

CITY Settlement larger than a town

CIVIC Relating to the duties of citizens and their governance

CITY BEAUTIFUL US architectural and town-planning movement, viewing cities as artworks

CITY STATE City forming an independent state

CLASSICAL Referring to the culture, art and architecture of ancient Greece and Rome

COLONIA Roman town establishing order in newly acquired territories

COLONNADE Columns placed at regular intervals supporting a horizontal roof; often fronting city shops

COMPREHENSIVE REDEVELOPMENT Post-war term signifying the wholesale destruction of historic town and city centres

CONSERVATION AREA An area of special architectural or historical interest protected by law

CONTEXTUALISM Building anew in the spirit of existing towns and cities

CONURBATION Cities merged into one another

COURT Area enclosed by buildings

DEFENSIBLE SPACE Architectural theory purporting that high-rise housing leads to high crime levels

DESIGN GUIDE 'House style' for new urban developments

ECO TOWN A town designed to be environmentally friendly

EDGE CITY Large newly developed area on the fringe of an existing city

EMBANKMENT Roads and other structures built over and alongside urban rivers

ESTATE Development owned by a single landowner

EYECATCHER Structure designed to animate vistas and skylines

FLÂNEUR Man of leisure who strolls idly along city boulevards in search of diversion

FOCAL POINT Structure placed at the end of a vista to draw the eye

FORUM Public space (Ancient Rome) associated with civic buildings

FREEWAY Wide road uninterrupted by cross streets, designed to speed traffic across cities

GARDEN CITY Ideal self-sufficient green city

GATED COMMUNITY Residential community protected by gates, walls and other security measures

GENTRIFICATION The smartening up of run down urban areas